8/10/80

For Clark Ellison

Best wishes always

Jim R. Griffie

Stepping Stones

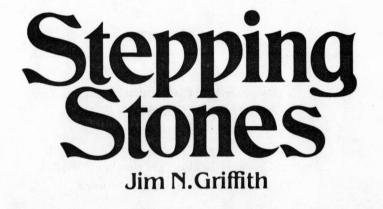

Stepping Stones

Jim N. Griffith

BROADMAN PRESS
Nashville, Tennessee

4252-79

ISBN: 0-8054-5279-6

Dewey Decimal Classification: 248.4
Subject heading: CHRISTIAN LIFE

Library of Congress Catalog Card Number: 79-55291
Printed in the United States of America

Unless otherwise noted, all Scripture quotations are from the King James Version of the Bible. Some biblical quotations are the author's interpretation and are so noted.

Scripture quotations marked GNB are from the *Good News Bible,* the Bible in Today's English Version. Old Testament: Copyright © American Bible Society 1976; New Testament: Copyright © American Bible Society 1966, 1971, 1976. Used by permission.

Scripture quotations marked NIV are from the HOLY BIBLE *New International Version,* copyright © 1978, New York Bible Society. Used by permission.

Scripture quotations marked Phillips are reprinted with permission of Macmillan Publishing Co., Inc. from J. B. Phillips: *The New Testament in Modern English,* Revised Edition. © J. B. Phillips 1958, 1960, 1972.

Dedicated to the memory of my parents, Benjamin Woodward Griffith, Sr., and Mary Norman Griffith, who first taught me what it meant to "step higher in faith"

Acknowledgments

Sincerest gratitude is expressed to all the courageous souls who, despite tremendous obstacles, have inspired me and others to march forward on the stepping stones of faith.

And to Mrs. Brinda Stanley who did her usual outstanding job in typing the final manuscript.

Contents

Contents

Preface

There is an old line of intended humor, aimed at the person who thinks he can do great wonders, which goes something like this: "Oh, he could walk on water—if he could locate the stones."

As is so often the case, there is a measure of truth in this humor. Fact is, we can "walk on the water," ford the turbulent streams—even cross the troubled seas of life—if we are willing to walk on the stones of faith and power available to us.

There are the stepping stones that will keep us on top of any situation. Contained in the pages of this book is the abundant life preserver for all who are struggling to survive stormy seas.

Here is an invitation for faltering feet to reach for something solid—support so strong and sturdy that we, like Simon Peter, can be prevented from sinking in the tempests of life.

Considered by some to be stumbling blocks, the following hardships are familiar to all: trouble, defeat, depression, loneliness, sorrow, impatience, pain, discouragement, and ever-present obstacles.

In reality, however, when viewed from the perspective of faith, these are not stumbling blocks but stepping stones. You recall that in his attempt to walk on water, the wind and waves did not cause Simon Peter to sink. He sank when he took his eyes of faith away from Christ, his all-sufficient source of sustaining strength.

So, as we move through these pages in faith, joy, and victory, let us resolve to use these stepping stones to march onward and upward to the higher way.

Jim N. Griffith

1
What to Do When It Rains

A longtime friend, dedicated Christian, and proud grandfather was visiting in his daughter's home. Everyone had gathered for breakfast: daughter, son-in-law, grandmother, grandfather, and the bright and sometimes outspoken four-year-old granddaughter.

As they sat down to eat, the young mother turned to her small daughter and said, "Barbara, why don't you say the blessing for us?"

Rubbing the sleep from her eyes, the tousled tot shyly refused, "But Mother, I don't want to say the blessing."

"All right, then," agreed her mother, "we'll ask Granddaddy to return thanks."

Eyes were closed; heads were bowed. Grandfather met the challenge of the occasion. He was so articulate that he even surprised himself. It was one of those rare moments when people felt that surely the angels in heaven must have put down their harps and paused to listen to this prayer.

Waxing eloquent, this veteran deacon thanked God for the food and then went into extensive expressions of gratitude for the beautiful day, the warm, bright sunshine, the deep blue sky, and all the beauty of God's good earth. On he went, his gratitude overflowing.

Finally, the blessing ended and everyone settled down to eat. Everyone, that is, but little Barbara. She looked thoughtful and contemplative. In a moment she spoke.

"Granddaddy," she blurted out, "Can I ask you something?"

"Why, yes, Honey," he said, "what is it?"

"Granddaddy," she asked, pausing for one additional brief second to reflect on his prayer, "What do you do when it rains?"

This was a good question. It is a good question for every child of man. What do you do when it rains?

What do you do or say when rain comes into your life? What do you do when the rains of trouble fall and the floods of tribulation rage? The Bible declares: "Man is born unto trouble, as the sparks fly upward" (Job 5:7). And it is true. Trouble is a part of life.

Art Buchwald, humorist and syndicated newspaper columnist, said in speaking at Boston's Emerson College: "Whether it is the best of times or the worst of times, it's the only time you've got."[1]

Sooner or later, trouble finds its way down every street and into every life. Inevitably, trouble arrives on the scene. And one acts, reacts, or takes it as it comes.

Somewhere I read about an old man who had been up to his neck in trouble all of his life. Yet he was always cheerful and contented. When asked the secret of his serenity, he replied: "I learned to cooperate with the inevitable."[2]

The sparks of trouble do fly upward, outward, and inward. Trouble enters often, and enters every area of our lives. Not the least of man's trouble in this day is the high cost of living. True, "man shall not live by bread alone" (Matt. 4:4), but he does not live at all without it.

The cost of providing food, housing, and medical service touches everyone. Some time ago in one of our large American cities a man was reported to have entered a hospital in a state of great agitation. Running about in a circle, he kept shouting: "I've got to see a psychiatrist! I've got to see a psychiatrist!"

"But," a friend reminded him, "*you* are a psychiatrist."

"I know," he answered, "but I charge too much."

Apparently, the cost of living hits everyone. The average man is in a continual struggle with the problem. Every time he almost gets to the point where he can make ends meet, somebody moves the ends.

Richard Armour expresses it well in this bit of verse:

> We had a little nest egg
> And watched it night and day,
> Until, as always happens,
> It hatched and flew away.[3]

Obviously, in the face of constant economic woes, the good old advice of "saving for a rainy day" is not the total answer. But still, this question demands an answer: What do you do when it rains, not cats and dogs but buckets of trouble, in your life?

When the rain comes down and the waters of difficulty start to rise around you, what is your reaction? Do you cry out, as did the prophet Ezekiel: "It was a river that I could not pass over: for the waters were risen, waters to swim in, a river that could not be passed over" (Ezek. 47:5).

And so, the question: What do you do when it rains? Do you watch for the rainbow and look for the sunshine? I am certain that we agree with Wordsworth that our hearts leap up when we behold a rainbow in the sky. It comes as a blessed assurance, for into every life at some time or other a little rain must fall. No matter how much we may try to escape, it will be sure to come.

There is the hard, bitter rain of disappointment and failure; the cruel rain of bereavement and sorrow; the cold, icy rain of sin and shame. It comes to all. The rain is no respecter of persons. Declare the Scriptures: "For he [your heavenly Father] maketh his sun to rise on the evil and on the good, and sendeth rain on the just and on the unjust" (Matt. 5:45).

Frequently the truth is that it never rains, but it pours; we encounter not one trouble but a sea of them. Although opportunity knocks on the door but once, trouble is more persistent.

With insight gained in their own experiences, there would be many who would identify with the lament from the words of Job: "Man that is born of a woman is of few days, and full of trouble" (Job 14:1).

Perhaps the most difficult thing to do, when the rain is falling heavily upon us, is to discern the rainbow shining through, to see the silver lining in the dark cloud. On the surface of our bitter circumstances, we see no purpose in our grief and sorrow and no rainbow of love peeping through the darkness that surrounds us.

"You ask me to believe in God," cries a father who has just lost his little boy in a shocking, fatal accident. "How can I believe in a God who allows such things to happen?"

Then, in the desolating and heartbreaking experiences of life, when the skies are so terribly overcast, we must trust where we cannot trace, believe that the rainbow is there—even though we cannot see it. Moreover, we must strive to understand that the meaning will ultimately appear if we but wait and trust and pray.

"Though he slay me, yet will I trust in him," said Job (Job 13:15). What a faith to display in the dark hours of the soul! When man can say that, we can see the rainbow beginning to shine through the clouds.

After all, even though there is no easy answer, there are answers to the hard questions of life. Man is eternally asking why it is true that, as the poet says, "Into each life some rain must fall." Why can we not live always in the light?[4]

Nature gives us the simplest answer: We could not grow that way. Put a seed out in the bright sunshine and nothing happens. It merely dries up and remains a seed. Bury the same seed in the dark earth, and it begins to climb and push its way toward the light. Finally bursting forth from its earthly prison, the seed unfolds and reaches upward toward the sunshine as it multiplies and increases.[5] In something of the same way, the dark days in an individual's life provide the necessary elements for the expansion and growth of the soul.

Rain, trouble, and difficulties that fall into every life

are not to be resented with harsh bitterness. They are not the Christian's permanent lot but are to be recognized as stepping stones leading to the development of what is highest and best in the heart of man.

No one in this world stands in the sunshine all of the time. We all have some shadows falling across our paths. The sky is not always blue—the sun does go under a cloud in everyone's sky. All of us must march through dark valleys. But life would be blessed and enriched if we came to realize that these patches of apparent darkness could provide the essential conditions for spiritual growth.

We often forget that if there were no rain, there could be no rainbow. Nature's masterpiece is formed by the rays of the sun being intercepted and broken by the drops of the rain. The clouds and rain form that beautiful bow of red, orange, yellow, green, blue, indigo, and violet which we view with wonder and delight.

I am certain you have observed that there are many persons—perhaps you are among them—who only begin to think of God and look for his rainbow when the merciless rain of difficulty is pelting down.

When things are going well, we consider ourselves among the favored folk who are enjoying blue skies and sunny days; we may entertain the foolish notion that we need no help from God. Later, however, as foul weather comes into our lives we can feel the brittle veneer of pride falling away and we are brought to the end of our self-sufficiency.

Three men lay dying in a hospital ward. Their doctor, making his morning rounds, went up to the first patient and asked him his last wish.

"My last wish," he murmured, "is to see a priest and make confession." The doctor assured him that he would arrange it and moved on to the next bed.

The second patient was asked his last request and he replied: "My last wish is to see all of the members of my family and say good-bye."

"It will be done," said the doctor as he turned away and continued his rounds.

The third patient was approached. "And what is your last wish?" the doctor asked.

"My last wish," came the feeble, hoarse reply, "is to see another doctor."

When serious difficulty comes into our lives, there are a great many persons who, in a very real sense, want another opinion. The verdict handed down by life may be a harsh one. Trembling hands reach out to grasp a thread of hope.

But the classroom of hard knocks ought to remind countless persons that again and again the exhausting rain of trouble has proved to be an excellent teacher. Just as the rain refreshes the barren countryside, trouble often proves beneficial to barren lives.

Many people would honestly admit that they have learned more from trouble than tranquility. A famous music teacher said of one of his pupils: "There is no doubt that she is a magnificent singer, and yet there is something lacking in her singing. Life has been too kind to her. But if somehow it happened that something broke her heart, she would be the finest singer of her day."

Trouble can equip us with that added dimension of a sympathetic touch. Our relationship with God can be made more real by hardship. Trouble, that relentless teacher, refines and polishes our character and humbles our ego.

In an incident recorded years ago, a young person was heard to say: "Would to God I had never been made!"

"Why, my dear child," replies a wise old woman, "you are not made yet. You are only being made, and you are quarreling with God's processes." It is an undeniable fact of life that fine steel cannot be made without the heat of the fire or outstanding character created outside the furnace of difficulty.

Van Wyck Brooks spoke the truth when he insisted that "the last straw may break the camel's back, but at least a large proportion of the other straws serve to develop its muscles."[6]

J. B. Phillips, the Bible translator, has a helpful paraphrase of 1 Peter 1:6-8: "At present, you are temporarily harassed by all kinds of trials. This is no accident—it happens to prove your faith, which is infinitely more valuable than gold, and gold, as you know, even though it is ultimately perishable, must be purified by fire. This proving of your faith is planned to result in praise and glory and honour in the day when Jesus Christ reveals himself."

These words come like a strong, reassuring hand

extended in times of turmoil. But let's face it: This does not alter the fact that many persons are frightened when they think about the shape the world is in and all of the associated problems that come with the package.

Someone has said that if Moses came down from Mount Sinai today, he would be carrying two additional tablets—aspirin tablets. Headaches are the order of the day for literally millions of persons. Pharmaceutical companies report that in each succeeding year the consumption of aspirin reaches a new high.

If not amusing, life is confusing. In some instances, *perplexing* is too tame a word to describe life as many now know it. Imagine this scene: Two cows are standing in the pasture. A milk truck approaches. On the side of the truck is a large printed sign which reads: "Fresh Milk, Standardized, Pasteurized, Homogenized, Grade A, Vitamins Added."

After the truck passes, one cow stops chewing her cud, turns to the cow next to her, and, with a worried look, says: "Kind of makes you feel inadequate, doesn't it?"

This is the way the submerged individual feels these days, as he finds himself sinking still deeper into the standardized, pasteurized, homogenized mass of trouble. Life in the present world situation is confusing. Half of the people seem to extol the virtues of "putting it all together" while the other half is busy taking it all apart. Although we may come to realize that burdens can be beneficial, we do not hold any great affection for them.

In these troubled days, there are many who feel that they have been saddled with unusually heavy burdens.

One woman said, "I know the Lord will not put more on me than I can bear, but I wish he did not have such a high opinion of me."

However, we easily overlook the troubles of others as we spend all of our time concentrating on our own problems. On one occasion when a delegation of complainers appealed to a discerning old man for encouragement in the troubles that plagued them, they were told to write on a piece of paper their most serious problems. The papers were then dropped into a box and each individual was instructed to draw a slip of paper. One by one they filed past, took a slip of paper, and began to read. Their faces reflected shock, terror, and grief. When they discovered the nature of their new trouble, which had been exchanged for the old, everyone clamored to have his own trouble back.

We never know what troubled waters others pass through until we have waded in their boots. A surprising truth is that those with the greatest problems issue the smallest number of complaints. In faith they have triumphed over trouble. They know that it is indeed wise to lay the good foundation in Christ before the rains come and beat upon the houses of their lives.

Eugene Pettyjohn, a pastor friend of mine, came by one afternoon to tell me that his sister, who lived in northwest Georgia, was scheduled to have surgery the next day.

"It looks serious," he said, as he sat across the desk from me. "I am afraid it is cancer."

Before he left, I suggested that we both get on our knees and pray that the God of all strength would equip his sister for any eventuality and bless her according to her every need.

We prayed and he left. Two days later we learned that his fears had not been without reason. Agnes, his sister, had cancer. The doctors had told her husband everything, not holding back any part of the bitter truth. "It was cancer and it had developed to the stage that there was nothing they could do." She could live, they said, from thirty days to a year at the most.

All of the members of her family were staggered by the news. But Agnes, on hearing the report from the operating room, was the calmest of all. This devout Christian had put down a good foundation in Christ before the rains came.

After she was dismissed from the hospital, Agnes returned home determined to be as active and productive as possible in the time that remained. She was not going to "pity" her time away. Neither did she plan to spend all of her time in bed, as long as she could get up and move around under her own steam. Friends and neighbors brought in fresh vegetables which she canned and prepared for the freezer. With a smile on her face and faith in her heart, she performed her daily household chores.

On one particular day she apparently went beyond the limit of her endurance. Exhausted, her physical strength gone, she dropped on the couch and began to pray: "Thank you, Jesus, for giving me the strength for this day."

"When I said that," she declared, "the presence of the Lord so filled the room that I could not keep from crying—his presence was so real—I felt him all about me!"

Regaining her strength, she went on to entertain her Woman's Missionary Union circle a few weeks later, marching in the strength of faith toward her inevitable sunset hour. When it rained in her life, she waited for the rainbow and looked for the sunshine—comforted by the knowledge that even when the sun is setting, the last rays of the sunshine belong to God.

If we know Christ as Lord and Master in time of good weather, we will not fail to see the rainbow glowing through the rain when it comes upon us. I once read of a terrible storm that blew into a coastal region. The wind howled around a little house in which a good old man was dying.

His daughter brought the family Bible to his bedside. "Father," she said, "I will read a chapter to you."

The old man was in dreadful pain and only moaned in answer. As she opened the Book to begin reading, the old man raised his hand and said, "No, no, Daughter. The storm is up now and I shall not live to see the sunshine again. But I'm glad to say that with the help of Almighty God, I patched my roof and thatched my house when the weather was calm."

Twice blessed is the man who can say that. He who calls Jesus, Master, under sunny skies will find that he is able to master every trial when the rains descend. So secure is he in his faith that he does not allow stormy weather to determine his attitude toward life.

One day, before leaving for school, a little boy finished his morning prayer with these words: "And we thank you, God, for this beautiful day." After he had said "Amen," his mother chided him for his seeming insincerity.

"It's not a beautiful day," said the mother, who reminded the child how cold, dark, rainy, and blustery it was outside.

"But Mother," replied the son, "it is a beautiful day." And then, with childlike insight he said: "Mother, don't ever judge a day by the weather!"

This is wisdom. Many of us are quick to render a harsh verdict on life because we look only on the surface and often view things from the wrong direction.

A chartered bus, transporting a tour group on an extended trip through the West, had stopped at a small hut in an Indian reservation where squaws sat cross-legged for many tedious hours weaving an intricate rug.

"I don't see why they work so hard to make a rug that looks like that," quipped a tourist. "It isn't at all pretty."

"Step around here," suggested the guide. "You are looking at it from the wrong direction."

When the tourist followed the suggestion, a beautiful array of color and design stretched out before him.

The troublesome events that happen in our lives, and in the world around us, often appear to have a tragic and heartless character about them—designed with an ugly pattern. Caught in the grip of such events, we sometimes find ourselves on the ledge of despair, but we must remember that we are looking at things from the underside.

The limits of our human horizons keep us from seeing the total picture. When God is at work, his designs and purposes are not always clear to us. But God is still at work, taking the tangled threads of life and weaving them into the beautiful fabric of his eternal design of good for us.[7]

When we look at life through the eyes of faith, we realize that life can be beautiful, regardless of the weather and the erratic design of circumstances. Every circumstance is filled with possibilities if one understands that trouble may prove to be only an opportunity in work clothes.

Aunt Sadie, my mother's younger sister, possessed this kind of outlook which resulted in a bright and indomitable spirit. Always jolly, she attracted children like a magnet. All of the children in the neighborhood gathered around her. In their sharp perception, the children saw a radiance that emerged despite the troubles in her own life. They liked to be near her, to bask in the light that hardship could not extinguish.

Her sense of humor was ever present. If the cupboard happened to be bare—which was not unusual in those depression years—she became a joking "old Mother Hubbard" who gathered her four children around her and made the best of the least. No matter what the crisis, she faced it with a smile.

During the time they lived in Atlanta, her oldest son was coming home from grade school one day when he heard the exciting sound of a siren on a fire truck approaching the neighborhood.

Running at top speed, he raced home, threw open

the front door and shouted, "Mother, can I go to the fire?"

Undaunted, a grin curving the corners of her mouth, she said, "Yes, I guess so, Buddy—the fire's in the kitchen!"

Experience has shown that many times, as in this case, the fire—the trouble—is located right in our own homes. Fortunately, the fire truck arrived in a moment at my aunt's house and the flames were put out with little damage. Nothing ever managed to quench the spirit of Aunt Sadie. Even if the wolf did camp on their doorstep during hard times, she would never let trouble get her down.

For Aunt Sadie, trouble was a stepping stone over which she walked as a composed, congenial conqueror. She did not bemoan the clouds or fret the rain. There was faith in her heart and a belief that life was to be lived and loved to the fullest.

Aunt Sadie would have echoed the good advice: "Don't judge any day by the weather." Instead we are to look at life through the beautiful window of joy and gratitude to God. "Casting all your care upon him; for he careth for you" (1 Pet. 5:7).

A story about Thomas Carlyle says that he was bothered by a rooster that would begin to crow early every morning. He talked to his neighbor, who owned the rooster, to see what might be done about the early bird.

"Does the crowing keep you awake?" inquired the neighbor.

"No," replied Carlyle. "It is not the crowing that

keeps me awake—it is my lying there in bed waiting for the rooster to crow!"

Beset by the problems of our day, it could be that many of us may be nervously tossing in our sleep waiting for the rooster of trouble to crow. But in the midst of nationwide difficulties, compounded by worldwide woes, we would do well to remember the word of a faithful old man to a small boy who was anxiously awaiting the dawn.

"Grandpa," the youngster asked, "won't the sun ever come up?"

"Well," Grandpa said, "it always has!"

What do you do in time of trouble? What do you do when it rains? You wait for God's sunshine—the everlasting light of his power and love.

2
You Can't Win 'Em All
(Or Can You?)

Some things in life are available to anyone who will accept them. Defeat is one of those things. But the important question is: Do you accept defeat or do you battle back and triumph over it?

This question cannot be ignored if one is to win in the contest of life. Do you use the vocabulary of victory or the vocabulary of defeat? The answer to this question is vital to your spiritual progress. It marks the dividing line between success and failure.

Among the most discouraging words one can hear are these: It can't be done. This is the attitude of the person who is ready to throw in the towel—even before the fight begins. However, the words that lift the heart and send you back into the battle are: It can be done!

After all, God wants each of us to trust unreservedly, to live abundantly, and to overcome triumphantly. The winner is one who bounces back after every blunder, comes back after every calamity, discovers diamonds after every disaster, mines miracles with every misfortune, and salvages success from every setback.

Unfortunately, the vocabulary of victory is seldom put into practice by many persons. But when these words are used, they provide the spark that brings glowing success. Experts in public relations consider the right attitude one of the most important aspects in achieving success in life. It is the "magic word" that produces excellent results in leadership and other phases of living.

William James, the most famous of all early American psychologists, said: "The greatest discovery of my generation is that human beings can alter their lives by altering their attitudes."[1]

Obviously many of us are shackled by speaking and thinking too much of difficulties and defeats and too little about the opportunities before us. The defeatist finds fault—the winner seeks a solution. The defeatist criticizes circumstances—the winner changes conditions. The defeatist disparages—the winner encourages. The defeatist erects barriers—the winner removes roadblocks. We would do well to remember that nothing can defeat us if we refuse to give up on the inside.

If for no other reason, we should at least want to be remembered for the smile of victory instead of the frown of futility, striving to live in such a way that when we pass on, we can avoid the epitaph: He Lived to a Gripe Old Age.

The surrender to defeat, which causes one to fold in the face of discouragement and turn sour on life, is a terrible blight on our day and age. Many are prone to overlook the joy that may be realized from capitalizing on calamity and turning defeat into victory.

A man who raised chickens in the basement of his house lived by a river that overflowed its banks one night, flooded the cellar, and drowned his prized hens.

He called his landlord and told him that he just had to move because the river flooded and drowned his chickens.

"Oh," said the landlord, "don't move on account of that. Try ducks!"

It is a great thing to be able to capitalize on calamity. This knack—this fortitude—for turning defeat into victory is needed all over God's good earth where life continues to suffer from an abundance of crepehangers.

From too many quarters the cry seems to be: "Things are bad now, but they are going to get worse!" Or, in other words, Cheer up—the worst is yet to come! In our compressed, condensed, compact age, everything has been shortened but some of the long faces.

One notable exception was the late United States senator from Minnesota. Hubert H. Humphrey never engaged in hand-wringing, breast-beating, and doleful prophecies. Even those who could not agree with his political philosophy had to admire the unconquerable spirit of the man.

After cancer had terminated his life and quieted that ebullient voice which had continued to ring out as pain gripped his body, a deacon in my church summarized his feelings about Humphrey with just a few words: "That Hubert Humphrey was some kind of man!" And he was all of that. These words came from one who never found political agreement with Humphrey, but the sheer courage of the senator—his unwillingness to accept defeat—had captured the admiration of this man.

To the extent that any man can be, Humphrey was deserving of the tributes he received, both as death was looming and then as it arrived. He deserved the tributes not only because of his office but also for the determination, zeal, and zest with which he tackled life.

Called the "Happy Warrior," Humphrey was accused of being too optimistic. But his kind of positive attitude was a needed antidote for the poison of pessimism that permeates so much of life today. Seemingly, the senator sought to live out in his life the words of the apostle Paul: "Work hard and do not be lazy. Let your hope keep you joyful, be patient in your troubles . . . Be happy with those who are happy, weep with those who weep. Do not let evil defeat you; instead, conquer evil with good" (Rom. 12:11-12,15,21, GNB).

Of course, the foregoing is not a plea for unfounded optimism. The world faces great crises. There are so many questions which man cannot answer. But if we persevere and continue in the strength that God provides, we can triumph over defeat.

There is one all-important question for which we do have an affirmative answer: Is God still in charge? Knowing that God does rule, we ought to move unswervingly toward the winner's circle, leaving behind us defeatist attitudes.

For, as that bit of anonymous verse explains it:

> If you think you are beaten, you are;
> If you think you dare not, you don't;
> If you'd like to win, but think you can't,
> It's almost a cinch you won't.

> If you think you'll lose, you've lost;
> For out in the world you'll find,
> Success begins with a person's will,
> It's all in the state of mind.
>
> Life's battles don't always seem to go
> To the strongest or wisest man,
> But sooner or later the man who wins
> Is the one who thinks he can.

Believing that one can win sets the tone for victory. There is a story told by Charles Allen of the barber in a small town who had been courting the librarian. For years the townspeople had watched as each afternoon he came by the library to walk her home.

On warm summer evenings they could be seen sitting together on her porch and in the cold of winter they would sit in the parlor. The town approved of the match and thought the couple was well suited for marriage, but the barber could never get up enough courage to pop the question.

Then one day a dashing, romantic salesman moved into the community. He went to check out a book from the library one day and, as is often the case, he became more interested in the librarian than in the library. More and more the salesman dropped around to check out books. One afternoon the librarian told the barber that she would be busy that night. To the barber's distress, she was busy on many nights that followed.

The entire town began to talk. The barber decided to discuss the matter with his friend, the pharmacist. The barber explained how much he loved the girl, that he wanted to marry her; but his courage failed him when it came time to ask her. The pharmacist reassured him and explained that he could fix him a capsule that would be just what he needed. The "courage" capsule was made and the barber was warned that it would act in a powerful way about fifteen minutes after he swallowed it.

The scene was set. That night he was to see the librarian. He took the capsule as he started to her house and by the time he got there his courage had so developed that he rushed in, threw his arms around his ladylove, and boldly announced, "Come on, we're going to get married!" And they did.

A few days later, the newly married man came by the drugstore and said to his friend, "That was the most powerful capsule I ever took. What was in it?" The pharmacist smiled and quietly replied: "Three things—first, a gelatin capsule; second, some sugar; and third, the belief that you could do it." The third ingredient was the one that mattered. Believing that you can do it is the ingredient that spells the difference between success and failure; victory and defeat. Great triumphs come to those who overcome little defeats.

We need to address ourselves to the task of overcoming defeat with the same kind of basic determination exhibited by a small boy learning to use a new pair of skates. He was falling so frequently and so hard that an onlooker said, "You are getting all banged up. Why don't you stop awhile and just watch the others?"

The lad paused only long enough to answer, "I didn't get these skates to give up on; I got them to learn on!"

Living in this world with all of its tumbles, falls, and hard knocks is a learning experience. The world is a great battleground of good and evil, righteousness and unrighteousness, defeats and victories. Ultimately we must come back to the basic nature of our faith: The Christian faith is not meant to provide an easy way of life. It is designed for tension, for conflict, for struggle, and for eventual victory. Even though the Christian may not always understand it, he seeks, in faith, to overcome life and its defeats.

As that famous network television news commentator says when he ends his program each day, "And that's the way it is." True, God could have given us an artificial victory. He could have created us as robots so that we would all march in a row and speak and act mechanically. No one would ever get out of step. Everything would be orderly, peaceful, and precise.[2]

Instead, God made us with minds and wills of our own. He gives us the opportunity to triumph and to accomplish worthwhile things, but not without conflict, not without paying a price. For there can be no triumph without conflict.[3] And the person who prays that God will shield him from all discord, disturbance, and danger is also praying to be shielded from victory.

Christianity is rooted in conflict which reached its climax at Calvary's Cross. But without that conflict, that apparent defeat, there could have been no resurrection, no triumph, and no hope of eternal life.[4]

Think of that which is worthwhile in your life—your children, your home, your job. Did these treasured possessions come easily? Was there a price to pay? Was there a struggle? Surely there was. And because of the struggle, there was the joy of victory, as experienced in this moving episode taken from real life.

I had finished speaking, stepped off the platform, and was greeting some of the people who had attended the spring revival meeting at a small-town church nestled in the north Georgia mountains. A man, his face lined from living many years, came from the choir loft, grabbed my hand and held it tightly. His eyes filled with tears, then overflowed, and spilled down his cheeks. "I wanted to stand up tonight," he said, "and thank God for answered prayer."

"That would have been wonderful," I replied, "we would have heard you gladly."

"You see," he went on, swallowing hard, "my wife and I have been praying for our son for twenty-two years. He has had all kinds of problems. But his mother and me—we never gave up—we wouldn't accept defeat— we kept on praying for him. And this weekend our prayers were answered."

I nodded as he paused a moment to get his emotions under control. "Our son came home—and it was like the return of the prodigal. He had received Christ and turned his life over to the Lord."

Rejoicing with this stalwart, old Christian, I was reminded of the stepping stone of prayer which can overcome defeat. During twenty-two years of stretching and straining in prayer, these faithful parents had reached for the answer to their breaking hearts and the answer had come.

Even apparent defeat can be turned into a stepping stone which can take us up and over the steepest mountains of life to triumph. The way may be long and hard, but prayer steadies our faltering feet, eases the load of our burdens, lifts our fainting hearts, and carries us on to conquest. With determination that springs from a firm faith, defeat can be exchanged for victory and one can capitalize on calamity.

Psalm 119 provides us with an example from God's Word. The psalmist is pictured as a man looking back upon his yesterdays. He was examining the way along which he had come. That way was not always through green pastures and beside the still waters. More than one tempest broke upon him. Treasures to which he clung were snatched from his hands and more than once his face was wet with tears.

But as he looked back upon those days of stress and strain, he realized that the final results had not been nearly as disastrous as he thought they would be. In fact, his losses became gain, his calamities changed into capital, and his defeats turned to victories.

"It is good for me that I have been afflicted" (v. 71), the psalmist cried in humble gladness. Although separated from the psalmist by centuries, we are like him in this respect: We all have our defeats—going through trying conflicts and being sorely wounded.

We are like the man who was struck by a bus and dragged three hundred feet along a busy street in New York City. Seriously injured, he was rushed to the hospital for emergency treatment. A few days later he regained consciousness with both legs bandaged and his arms in splints. A nurse asked him: "Are you comfortable?"

"Well," he replied, "I make a living."

Even this is not always easy to do in today's world. Life is so complex that it is difficult to make our way. As the story goes, the Lord came and told Moses he had good news and bad news: "You can lead your people out of Egypt through the parting of the Red Sea, but you will have to file an environmental impact study before the six o'clock deadline." Actually, Moses had more serious problems than ecology—as most people do. Still, God is sufficient. As the church bulletin board advised: "Bring Your Used Cares to the Lord. He Will Give You a Good Deal."

Having experienced all manner of conflict in his life, but knowing in full measure the love and strength of God, one sturdy old man declared: "When I face life's great computer, it can be said that although I was spindled and mutilated, I did not fold."

The joyful truth is that some do not fold in the midst of life's setbacks. They do not accept defeat. A minister shared with me the inspiring account of a young woman who would not take the line of least resistance and come to an easy acceptance of the defeat which hovered around her life due to a serious crippling disease. As a child, she had suffered a crippling bout with polio which had left her paralyzed on her left side. There had been long, painful stays in the hospital at Warm Springs, Georgia, followed by return trips for therapy and instructions on how to use the braces which she would be required to wear for the remainder of her life.

The paralysis was so severe that she could not get out of bed unless the braces were in place and securely fitted on both legs by her mother. The brace on her left side, which extended all the way to her shoe, would bend at the knee only after she snapped a release. It was so constructed that when she stood, the brace would automatically drop into place.

Yet, within this heavy harness, this young girl pushed on to graduate from high school. The minister, who was asked to deliver the baccalaureate address at her graduation exercises, watched as she marched in with the other graduating seniors.

The braces made a clicking noise as she approached the high steps leading to the platform. Mounting the steps, she struggled with the steep ascent, lost her balance for a second, steadied herself, jumped up the last step and came to her seat with a smile as though nothing had happened.

Following graduation, she was employed by the county agent's office where she did general office work—typed and operated the mimeograph machine —mostly with her one "good hand."

It was not long after this that her mother died, joining her father who had passed on some years earlier. Now there was no one to fit the braces and give her a boost out of bed in the morning. On the surface, this cruel additional handicap seemed to spell defeat. But not so. This young woman not only had faith. She had fortitude and ingenuity.

Through dogged determination, she would keep struggling each morning until she worked herself into the braces and out of bed. And it is to her everlasting credit that her victories did not stop with that one.

In later years, she was married to a fine young man and to this union was born a beautiful baby girl. In her heroic life, this young mother personified faith and determination as one who, when down, would not be counted out. She marched with all those brave souls who would not allow themselves to be defeated by defeat.

But since defeat is so nearly a universal human experience, the question that clamors for an answer is this: What are you going to do about it? Sadly, there are some who have the attitude of going under. They dig a hole of self-pity, fall in, and pull the dirt of submission around them. They are ready to give up the fight at the very first painful injury they receive in the battle of life. Having fallen, instead of rising to their feet to renew the struggle, they lie down and bewail their hard lot. Without a change of attitude, they spend their remaining days as spiritual invalids. They shut themselves in with their defeat.

The same tragic blunder was made by Miss Havisham in the book, *Great Expectations* by Charles Dickens. She was to be married, you remember. The guests were gathered. The wedding feast was prepared. The wedding cake was on the table. The bride was decked in her bridal gown. But the bridegroom never came. Therefore, her watch, and every clock in the house, was allowed to stop at twenty minutes until nine—the hour of her humiliation, the hour of her first and one great sorrow.

All sunlight was shut out of Miss Havisham's home. She lived in the dark except for the light of candles. Her wedding cake remained on the table until cobwebs surrounded it. For her, all life had stopped at the hour of her tragic disappointment. She had met her defeat with unconditional surrender.

The way of surrender is not the way of faith. A man was talking one day to John Wesley and saying that he did not know what he could do with his perplexities. The two were passing a meadow bounded by a stone fence, over which a cow was looking.

"Do you know," asked Wesley, "why that cow looks over the wall?"

"No," said the man.

"I will tell you," Wesley explained, "it is because she cannot look through it. And that is just what you must do with that which would hinder you—look over and above it."

By looking over and above defeat and seeing God, man can avoid the pitfall of allowing difficulties to make him hard and cynical. Thus strengthened, he can ignore the notion that everything is going to ruin. It is a reflection of human nature that many are quick to believe in the goodness of God when all goes right; but if things go wrong, they have other thoughts.

Similarly, the cricket in the spring builds his little house in the meadow and chirps with joy because things are going so well with him. But when he hears the sound of the plow a few furrows off, and the roar of the tractor's motor almost upon him, then the skies begin to look dark. The plow comes crunching along and turns his dwelling place bottom side up, and as he goes rolling over and over without a home, he says, "Oh, the foundations of the world are destroyed and it is going to ruin!"

In many ways, we are like the cricket. If anything happens to overthrow our plans, we think all is going to ruination. But the heartening fact is that the furrow where the plow has been will be replaced with growth and an eventual harvest of blessings to those who wait for another day.

All those who refuse to surrender to their defeats either by turning coward or becoming calloused and hard shall ultimately capitalize on their calamities and change their losses into gains. They know that affliction can strengthen Christian graces. "Tribulation worketh patience" (Rom. 5:3).

And we often learn more under the rod that strikes us than we do under the rod that comforts us. Events frequently afford us the privilege of being in the inspiring presence of someone who has let tribulation weave a praiseworthy patience into the frustrating fabric of his life.

"I like all sports, but only as a spectator, of course," declared the young man with a cheery smile. One glance in his direction told you why. He was in a wheelchair and had been for thirty of the thirty-four years of his life.

In the finest sense of the word, Larry Mauldin is an "active" member of the County Line Baptist Church in

Philomath, Georgia. This was verified for the supply pastor who had gone to speak at Larry's church, as he watched the young man being rolled into the Sunday School department where he taught a class of twelve-year-old boys.

Following the morning worship service, the visiting minister was invited to eat the noon meal at the Mauldin home. After lunch, Larry asked the visitor if he would like to see his room. As they entered, the pastor could not hide his astonishment at what he saw. He had not expected to see an iron lung in one corner of the room. Larry smiled and said simply, "This is where I sleep every night." The iron lung had been obtained five years before when the young man suffered a severe respiratory problem which almost claimed his life.

In the course of the afternoon conversation, the preacher also learned that Larry had served his church from his wheelchair as both Sunday School and Church Training director and was now spending every Sunday morning teaching a class of boys about the love of Jesus. This frail, yet radiant Christian—so willing to dedicate all that he has to the service of his Lord—exemplifies persons of championship caliber who take whatever life has to offer and then go on to triumph over defeat.

Those who have been to the land of broken hearts—those who have been to school in Gethsemane—are the most helpful, inspiring people I know.

Some years ago, while speaking in revival services in a small Southern town, I went with the host pastor to visit a woman who had been an invalid for over ten years. Struck down with a dread crippling disease, she had to spend her remaining earthly days confined to bed.

Her hands, which once played the organ in her church so beautifully, were now twisted, drawn, and gnarled like the branches of a tree that had been punished by harsh windstorms. But her face—her face was as bright as the rising sun. Her spirits were not dampened but bore witness to the fact that she found her strength in God.

From the standpoint of every person who has ever dealt with defeat, the good news for you and me is this: We, too, can learn the secret of capitalizing on calamity. Let it be underscored that we must believe in the possibility of changing our losses into gains. Almost two thousand years ago the apostle Paul desired to preach the gospel in Rome. But he was thrust into jail where he remained for long, weary months. Nevertheless, in writing a letter from prison, he said: "I would ye should understand, brethren, that the things which happened unto me have fallen out rather unto the furtherance of the gospel" (Phil. 1:12).

The word "furtherance," as translated from the Greek, means to "advance or drive forward" which, in itself, is an inspiring thought. "All of these defeats that have come upon me," Paul was saying, "have served instead to drive forward the gospel of Christ." Beyond that, on his way to Rome, the apostle was shipwrecked. But even this did not sink his spirits.

Furthermore, Paul had a thorn in the flesh. He insistently went to God and pleaded for its removal (2 Cor. 12:7). The painful nature of this adversity is confirmed in the interpretation of the word from the original tongue which describes the thorn as a pointed piece of wood, a stake that would pierce flesh—indicating a constant bodily ailment or infirmity.

But be that as it may, the Lord refused his request, saying: "My grace is sufficient for thee" (2 Cor. 12:9). And Paul lived to thank God, even for his thorn: "Most gladly therefore will I rather glory in my infirmities, that the power of Christ may rest upon me" (2 Cor. 12:9). Paul not only had the power of God resting upon him but also the love of God surrounding him.

In his book, *The Father Is Very Fond of Me,* Ed Farrell tells the story of a young priest who was enjoying a late afternoon walk one day in Ireland when he came across an old man who was also out enjoying the stillness of nature in the waning afternoon hours. As they walked along together, it started to rain, and they took shelter in a nearby shed.

They talked for a while; but when the conversation dwindled into silence, the old man took out a prayer book and began reading from it half aloud. After some minutes, the priest said: "You must be very close to God," and the old man replied: "Yes, he is very fond of me."[5]

This story pulls back the curtain on a thrilling revelation of God's grace and love. Our heavenly Father is very fond of us, and his love is not dependent on anything we do. God plainly, simply, and completely loves us. God's grace is not based on how much we love him but on how much he loves us.[6]

And in the strength of God's love and grace, many of his children, through the ages, have been equipped to face defeat and turn tragedy into triumph. "Through all that I have suffered," Joseph of the Old Testament could say, "God has been on my side and has brought me through to victory" (Gen. 50:20, author's translation).

This is the thrust of what missionary Verena Hekman is saying:

Think of yourself in Joseph's place:
—heading in a caravan south
—hot, smelly traders
—language unintelligible
—road map unavailable
—destination unknown
—communications cut with family
—dreams broken
—lost his prize coat, a favorite son's insignia
—(little did Joseph know, that he would get another "coat" years later that was fit for a king!)[7]

Faith in God is the only power that can enable a man to accept his lot in life and go from there to ultimate success, in spite of every defeat.

One time in a golf tournament a famous golfer had a "bad lie." He hit a tremendous drive down the fairway, but the ball took a bad hop and landed in the rough. A spectator standing nearby said, "What a shame; that's not fair. You shouldn't have to play it from there."

The golfer replied, "That's where the ball is."

Obviously, that is not only a great thing to say about golf but also a great thing to say about life. Faith in God will enable you to play life where it is.

Joseph did just that. He had been knocked off the fairway into the rough of life. But with a deep trust in God, he was able to get a boost from his knocks and triumph over defeat. So it is when a life is dedicated and consecrated to God. Joseph had suffered much. He was sold into slavery, falsely accused, and imprisoned. But from this, he emerged as the most powerful man in Egypt. And Joseph was able to do this because he walked with God every step of the way and refused to raise the white flag of defeat.

Those who win are those who never give up. Winston Churchill said the secret of success is in these six words: "Never, never, never, never give up." These words helped bring Churchill through the uncertain days of World War II. And for all persons who have their own private wars and battles in life, be assured that those who are victorious are those who never surrender.

When William Booth, the founder of the Salvation Army, was told he was going blind, he asked his son, "So you mean that I am to be blind and must remain blind?"

"I am afraid it is so," answered his son.

This great old Christian then reached out his hand

until he clasped the hand of his son and said, "God must know best. I have done what I could for God and the people with my eyes. Now I shall do what I can for God and the people without my eyes." Such an attitude of determined faith is equal to any situation, come what may.

> It can change tragedy into triumph,
> Calamity into capital,
> Grief into gain,
> Darkness into light,
> Tears into joy,
> And defeat into victory.

3
Depressed?

This is the age of humanity's frantic search for happiness. For our weary and depressed generation, happiness is more elusive than the proverbial "pot of gold" at the end of the rainbow. And all indications are that man's will to be happy has weakened. As J. Harold Smith said: "All you have to do to hatch despair is to just brood over your troubles."[1]

Look at this picture: A physician and a stranger are together in the examination room. The doctor is talking to this troubled man whose countenance bears lines of deep despair.

"As long as you are depressed and unhappy you will be ill," says the doctor.

"I know," the man agrees, "but how can I cure this depression?"

The doctor answers, "There is a circus performing in town today. I always like to be there for the opening performance. The clown, who is with the circus, always makes me laugh. Please be my guest for the circus. If you want to laugh, this clown can help you."

In the staring eyes of his patient, the doctor noticed tears forming. "No," the patient said, "I do not believe the clown can make me laugh. You see, Doctor, I am that clown."

Happiness is an elusive thing. Some cannot hold on to it. Happiness slips through their fingers and out of their lives. And, like the clown, others wear a mask of happiness, but deep inside—down where they live—they are depressed. Whatever else this may be, it is certainly not God's plan for the Christian. Joy is mentioned more than seventy times in the New Testament. The Scriptures record the joy of salvation, the joy of contentment, and the joy of service.

Paul, in writing to the church at Philippi declared, "Rejoice in the Lord alway: and again I say, Rejoice" (Phil. 4:4). This is interpreted to mean, "Rejoice exceedingly, be glad, and be well." After all, no one is a better advertisement of any product than a satisfied customer; Christians ought to be satisfied, contented, and joyful customers. Nevertheless, many Christians are poor examples of genuine joy. Their desperate hearts do not possess true joy. For too long they have allowed their faith to be more of a form than a force.

Paul, warning young Timothy, said there are many "having a form of godliness, but denying the power thereof" (2 Tim. 3:5). A better translation might be: "Though they keep up a religious front, they will have nothing to do with the power of faith." Consequently, more people today have some religious connection. At the same time there appears to be less happiness and more depression.

Although America is perhaps the only nation in the world where the individual has the freedom to pursue happiness, the lack of sufficient mental and emotional happiness results in 15 percent of America's population experiencing serious depression at some point in their lifetime. Deep depression is not to be confused with the less serious but more prevalent blahs that seem to affect almost everyone at one time or another. Blahs are apparently more common on rainy days, but this is not always the case. "Drabitis," boredom, depression—whatever label you want to give it—can attack even when the sun is shining brightly.

Most persons experience certain periods of depression which cause them to consider folding their hands and giving up. The fact is, depression is a nondiscriminatory disease that attacks Christians as well as non-Christians, the religious as well as the nonreligious. Persons of every age group, financial level, and social status are victims of depression. The case records show that not even ministers and their wives are immune.

Some people live under the misconception that once they accept Christ as Lord and Savior, all of their troubles are over. This is contrary to real life and to the teachings of the Bible. "In the world ye shall have tribulation: but be of good cheer; I have overcome the world" (John 16:33).

Therein is the difference that Christ can make. Everyone will experience a certain amount of trials and troubles that can lead to depression, but the plus for the Christian is that he has a loving and merciful Lord who "has overcome the world" and stands ready to help in time of need.

It was well past midnight and still the old man,

caught in the clutches of depression, could not sleep.

"It's hopeless—this world of ours is doomed," he moaned. Then, suddenly, he seemed to hear a voice speaking in the darkness. It was, he felt, the voice of God, speaking to him, saying: "Go to sleep, old man. I will sit up the rest of the night."

Taking your burdens to the Lord, as the old hymn advises, and leaving them there is wise counsel. Anxiety and depression never baked a cake, built a bridge, won a battle, or solved a problem. Actually, we render ourselves far less useful if we let worry and depression stall our action.

The best thing we can do is work, with all of our strength, on the opportunities God gives us and then leave the final outcome to the divine Director. Should we ever give in to our depression? Not according to the Scriptures:

> Nay, in all these things we are more than conquerors through him that loved us. For I am persuaded that neither death, nor life, nor angels, nor principalities, nor powers, nor things present, nor things to come, nor height, nor depth, nor any other creature, shall be able to separate us from the love of God, which is in Christ Jesus our Lord (Rom. 8:37-39).

The ability to be a conqueror is not in us but in Christ who makes us "more than a conqueror" in all things. A group of college students was attending a conference where one young person from each state was participating in a speaker's tournament. During the time set aside for preparation for the speaker's tournament, one young woman, who was very short, checked the microphone and found that it was at least a foot above her head. Attempting to adjust it, she found that she could not. Alarmed, she ran to the person in charge and shouted, "The mike is too high!" The leader, with a well-known sense of humor, smiled and calmly declared: "You have fifteen minutes in which to grow."[2]

The suggestion not withstanding, most of us can identify with the anxiety of this young woman. When faced with the world and all of its problems and our own sense of inadequacy in meeting the demands of the situation, we may have a strong desire to run to our heavenly Father and in panic shout, "The problems are too tall for me. Lower them so I can handle them."

Yet, reason reminds us that this is not the way God helps us. He does not shrink the problems of life to the smaller size of our abilities. No. God strengthens and reinforces his children so that they will be "more than conquerors" in the living of these days.

Being a victorious Christian in today's world requires more than we have, but it does not require more than is available in God. The stifling, depressing, imprisoning experiences of life—when faced in the power of God—may become the means of strong and healthy growth.

Nearly twenty centuries ago the apostle Paul was cast into prison when it seemed that he was urgently needed in a score of places. But now, seen in the light of the intervening years, we know that his imprisonment advanced the cause to which he was devoted. The letters to the Philippians, Colossians, Ephesians, and Philemon were all written during this period of Paul's life. He lived long enough to see that the imprisoning experience was not depressive but expansive.

It was the same with the psalmist who said: "Thou hast enlarged me when I was in distress" (Ps. 4:1). As the psalmist drew near to the unwelcome circumstances, his face was covered with a frown. The situation seemed to cripple and belittle. But it turned out to be the means of his enlargement. It had appeared to shut him in, when it was, in reality, opening him out. He was enlarged when he was in distress.

Indications are that this is one of the laws of life. A wealthy man once received as a present a valuable plant, the nature and habits of which were unknown to him. The plant was given to the care of the gardener, who supposing it to be a tropical plant, put it in the hothouse and treated it like other hothouse plants. Under this treatment the plant began to wither and die.

One day a horticulturist came by and while there he was asked to examine the ailing plant. As soon as he had done so, he said: "Your trouble is obvious. This is an arctic plant, and it is being killed by this hothouse treatment." The plant was placed in the open air and ice piled around it. To the astonishment of all, the plant soon became healthy and strong.

This incident is a parable of human character. It is ease—not difficulty that is dangerous. Place a man under hothouse treatment. Surround him with luxury and ease. Protect him from all opposition. That is the surest way to sap him of life and power. As the psalmist said: "Thou hast enlarged me when I was in distress" (Ps. 4:1).

This formula will not work unless we make up our minds and hearts to look upon the hard experiences of life as expansive rather than depressive. A young woman lay critically injured, following a grinding automobile accident. After several weeks in the hospital, she impatiently asked the doctor: "How long must I lie helplessly on this hospital bed?"

The wise doctor replied: "Just one day at a time."

This is excellent advice. Before giving in to despair and depression, let us look again at what it means to live one day at a time. Faith says, "Let us go on. Yesterday is gone. Tomorrow is not here. Today is all we have. We will accept it and make the best of it—one day at a time."

Make these words your words: This is a new day. I can waste it or use it for good. What I do today is important because I am exchanging a day of my life for it. When tomorrow comes, this day will be gone forever, leaving something in its place which I have traded for it. I want it to be gain, not loss; good, not evil; success, not failure.

If we use each day as God would have it, each day will be a growth experience. A few years ago at a small Eastern college, a young professor with only two years of teaching experience was made chairman of the department of English. An older professor, who had been in the English department for twenty-two years, was displeased with the appointment and went to talk with the college president to determine the rationale behind the decision. During the conference, the professor asked the president to explain how he could justify passing over a man with twenty-two years of experience and elevating a man with only two years of experience.

The president's answer was classic: "You are in error, Sir. You do not have twenty-two years of teaching experience. You have only one year's teaching experience twenty-two times!"

This opens up a pertinent question for you and me. Are we growing? Are we gaining anything from our day-to-day, month-to-month, and year-to-year experiences? Or could it be that we are just repeating the same old year over and over again?

Ask yourself the question: Am I growing, am I being enlarged in my distresses? An eccentric farmer built a fence that measured four feet high and five feet wide. When asked why he decided to build a fence with such unusual dimensions, he replied: "Well, in case a strong wind blows it over, it will be higher than it was to start with." Life has a way of blowing over our fences. But if we allow our Lord to enlarge us in our distress, we can be bigger or higher than we were to begin with.

True, there are times when the whole world appears determined to rain on our parade and the winds of adversity do blow our fences over. Even so, we can bend with the breezes; we do not have to break. Problems and distresses are what they are, but God is who he is. And with God's assistance, we can live the words of a popular song of many seasons ago: You can "be better [and bigger] than you are."

Asked the secret of her serenity and joy in life, an elderly woman explained, "I make the most of what comes and the least of what goes." This determined lady was putting into practice one remedy for depression. Through lean and fat years, encounters with good and bad folk, she has chiseled out her own wonderful life-style whereby she accentuates the positive; eliminates the negative; maximizes the good; and minimizes the bad.

Untold multitudes are in need of assuming this positive stance in life. Depression is so much a part of today's scene that if you stopped almost one out of every four persons on the street, you might hear something like this: "Yes, there was a time when life was moving in broad, quiet waters of happy experiences and the glow of contentment filled our hearts from morning until night, but then life became suddenly complicated. We found ourseleves entrapped in distress."

This is an apt description of what took place in the lives of two friends of mine. I had known them for over twelve years and had shared in the joys of their life. An outstanding professional man, he had a good income and all the attendant blessings. Even so, the spiritual had not been neglected in their family. All were Christian, both parents and children. Their church meant much to them. When the doors opened for services, they were there. Life was good.

Then, swiftly and tragically life fell in on them. One child developed a serious and chronic disease that would require lifelong care and treatment. Another child was injured in an accident. The husband's mother was operated on for cancer. The wife's mother died after months of failing health. Still, this fine couple did not shrivel up and quit. They endured. It was terribly difficult, but with faith and perseverance, they kept their heads above waters of depression for a long time.

However, there would be more—much more to try their faith. The husband himself became ill and entered the hospital for surgery. I arrived early the morning they took him down to the operating room and prayed with him, his wife, and mother. While the surgery was in progress, a host of friends came to show their concern for this man and his wife who had done so much for others through the years. The operation did not last as long as we had anticipated which, in this case, was bad news.

The wife was pale and shaken as the surgeons came up to give her the verdict from the operating room: "It was bad news—about as bad as it could be. A malignant tumor we could not get to, near the brain."

The news was all the wife had not wanted to hear, but she listened as the doctors told her they would refer her husband to a large hospital where doctors specialized in this type of cancer surgery.

The bad news hit like a collapsing building and fell all around us: "The patient would lose an eye in radical surgery. There was no way to say at this point just how successful further surgery and treatment would be."

Family members trembled with grief. Dazed, they found it hard to believe, but they pushed on with the things that had to be done. Arrangements were made for the transfer to the cancer center in Houston, Texas, and surgery followed. It was "radical" in the harshest sense of the word.

After a period of convalescence, they flew home for a few days before cobalt treatment was scheduled to begin at the tumor institute in Houston. We went by to welcome him home and while we were there, his wife who had been through so much in sharing the burden of her husband, said: "I want to see you and talk to you while I am here."

She came to the office the next day. I stood to greet her, motioned her to a chair, and said: "Well, how are you?"

"That's what I want to talk to you about," she said. "I've got some bad feelings about all of this. I have terrible resentment in my heart—resentment against all of our difficulties, resentment against this illness. I am not blaming God, but I am just filled with resentment and it is pulling me down."

"That's exactly what resentment will do," I said. And then I shared a learning experience I had a few years ago while conducting a revival meeting in a south Georgia city.

As the visiting speaker, I was entertained for lunch in the home of a physician who, for some years, had been a general practitioner and then had felt led to become a psychiatrist. Returning from special training, he set up practice in the same community. He was a dedicated

Christian, a man with concern and caring for the problems of others.

"I am sure," I said, "with my pastoral counseling, we must come across some of the same situations. One of the hardest problems to deal with is depression. So many now are struggling in the pit of depression. Could you give me some insight at this point?"

The doctor looked thoughtful for a second and then said: "Depression is perhaps the biggest problem I deal with."

"I am sure," I agreed, "that many pastors could echo that. But tell me—what do you think is the greatest cause of depression in most people?"

The psychiatrist answered, "Past studies and numerous case histories have shown that, in most instances, depression is caused by resentment. Someone has a deep resentment against an illness, a misfortune, a setback on the job; the result is depression."

After sharing with my friend this wisdom of the Christian psychiatrist, I advised: "Now you see what resentment will do for you—it can only depress you."

She nodded and said, "I know this is true—but I get so full sometimes with this hurting inside that I feel as if I may overflow."

"Well," I said, softly, "go ahead and overflow. You are due some tears. But do not let resentment push you off the cliff of depression. The jolt is too rough when you hit bottom."

Blotting at her eyes with her handkerchief, she swallowed hard and nodded in agreement.

"Strange as it may sound," I continued, "when the

Christian works through resentment and turns it over to the Lord, it can be a stepping stone to a higher spiritual way. And when this giant step is taken, the all-sufficiency of God's grace is available to meet every desperate need of life."

Before this friend left my office, we prayed to the God of all comfort that he would walk with her and her husband through the valley of depression and lead them out on the other side to the higher, happier way.

Inasmuch as resentment is a major cause of depression, note these tips on handling resentment: Don't face the wrong way. The word *resent* comes from two Latin words meaning "to feel back." Resentful people are often those who live in the past. What did Paul tell us? "This one thing I do, forgetting those things which are behind, and reaching forth unto those things which are before, I press toward the mark for the prize of the high calling of God in Christ Jesus" (Phil. 3:13-14).

Remember: A resentful individual is captured by an emotion and in bondage to an emotional reaction. Choose to surrender your feelings to Christ and elect to have your freedom. Take a positive position. If you have committed everything to "the Lord who doeth all things well," then you will find it easy to take the final step; forgive and forget.

In winning out over depression, attitude is all important. The story is told of a woman who, during World War II, went to live with her husband in camp on the Mojave Desert in New Mexico. She simply hated the place. She resented everything about it: The heat was almost unbearable—105 degrees in the shade—and there was sand—sand everywhere. Finally, she was so depressed that she wrote her parents in Ohio. She could not stand the desert another minute and was coming home. By return mail, she received a quick reply from her father that contained just two familiar lines:

"Two men looked out from prison bars,
One saw mud, the other saw stars."

The daughter did some hard thinking not only with her mind but also with her heart. She decided to stick to her post. Making friends with the natives, she learned to love the country, and eventually wrote a book about it. The desert had not changed, but her attitude had. Because she listened with her heart to the words her father had sent, a new and exciting world opened up to her.[3]

We usually see what we look for. Two men stand outside, looking skyward. One comments on the dark cloud—the other praises the warm sunshine. There is truth here. Many are miserable and incapacitated for daily living because they only look on the dark side of life. This is not to say that life does not have its depressing setbacks. Doors are closed before and behind us. We seem to be closed in. And then, the waters of life come, and we begin to rise.

When God, the merciful Guardian who watched over Israel, opens the forward gate and restores our freedom, we begin to know what has happened. Life opens out in larger reaches. "Thou hast enlarged me when I was in distress" (Ps. 4:1), said the psalmist.

People grow larger in their sorrows and difficulties. A

man who had never been sick before and suddenly found himself flat on his back said, "My, but things look different from the horizontal!" It is a fact proven countless times that we struggle through difficulties to the higher life of the Spirit. One who is depressed can, in the Spirit of Christ, let his resentment be a presentment for growth.

I have read somewhere that men who look up from the bottom of a deep pit can see the stars at noon. I do not know if this is true, but I do know that when men and women are sunk in the pit of adversity and look up, stars of promise come out to bring them cheer.

In a Singapore prison, following the outbreak of World War II, there was a prisoner whose best friend had been sentenced to solitary confinement by the Japanese. He wondered what he could do to help his friend. The obvious answer was *nothing.* His friend was locked up in a tiny cell in a section of the prison which was so heavily guarded that no one could get in without special permission.

Then one day a fellow prisoner saw this man trying to cut another prisoner's hair. "John," he said, "I never knew you could cut hair!"

"I can't," replied John. "It is something I've never done before. I'm just learning. As you know, my friend is in solitary. He is allowed to have his hair cut once a month. So I thought I'd apply for the job."

Sometime later all the prisoners heard that John had been appointed as barber for those in solitary. He was asked, "How are things working out now that you see your friend, Jim, every month?"

John answered: "Oh, all right. Of course, I can't take him anything and I am not allowed to talk to him. But while I'm snipping away at his hair, I can keep saying to him, 'Please keep your chin up. Don't forget to keep your chin up.' The guards think this had something to do with barbering—a shibboleth of the trade. So I just keep saying 'Chin up! Chin up!' "[4]

And this is what our loving Lord comes to say to us. He comes to us in our imprisonment, offering the way out of our maze of dreary, depressing days and says: "Chin up! Chin up! Do not despair. There is hope."

4
Alone? Never!

Loneliness is a widespread disease of our day. Clearly, there is no vaccine for it. In most instances, there is no immunity from it.

A woman from Ohio, in December of 1969, wrote a touching letter to the postmaster in Nashville, Tennessee. She enclosed twenty-five cents in coin and made a strange request.

"Please, will someone in Nashville use this quarter to send me a Christmas card?"

This woman lived alone in poverty. She had never married and had no near kin. Confined to her home with a leg injury, she had been forced to quit her job at a laundry. For Christmas, she asked only that someone in a strange and distant city send her a greeting card.

Loneliness is very real to the aged, who have outlived most of their relatives and friends or who are separated by long distances. Loneliness is also prevalent with those who are not good at making friends. And loneliness is often disturbing even to those who live in the heart of the largest cities in the world.

One story, in what would be millions of similar circumstances, is of the elderly lady in Atlanta who phones the correct time service every night just before going to bed.

Someone asked her if she had a clock.

"Yes," she answered, "of course, I have a clock, but I call every night, not because I want to know the time, but just to hear somebody's voice before I go to bed."[1]

Loneliness is an awful condition. It could be described as the feeling of being broke, with no money, in the midst of a room full of rich relatives. But the truth is, it is worse than that. Many are as lonely, Byron said, "as a single cloud on a sunny day, while all the rest of heaven is clear."

Adding to the seriousness of the problem is the fact that loneliness afflicts so many. Even ministers are not immune. John Claypool tells of receiving a telephone call from a fellow clergyman in a neighboring church. There was desperation in his voice as he asked a searching question: "Where does a pastor go for pastoral care?"[2]

He went on to say that he was calling five pastors and asking if they would meet in his office and be a part of a support group. "I do not know if this will work," he said, "but this is my last hope."

The minister was in dire straits. He was walking the lonely path of desperate need. Admitting his need, he was openly reaching out for help from another. Claypool said, "I was going through considerable personal turmoil in my own life just then. I was really suffocating in the loneliness and isolation into which I had thrust myself, and part of me instinctively leaped for joy at the idea of such a support group."[3]

The results of the support meetings were shocking. Almost every man around the table, who appeared to be so outwardly competent, was also having to struggle with the inward feeling of loneliness.

Masks were removed and "band-aids of pretense" used to hide serious wounds were stripped away. Hurts were seen and felt and shared. Honest confession was followed by honest compassion and support. They experienced grace. Emerging from their loneliness, they knew, in a more glorious way than ever before, the support of man and the grace of God. Loneliness had become a stepping stone to the higher way.

This was also true in the life of an active Tennessee church leader, Mrs. Sibley Burnett. She tells her own story:

Several times in our lives we come to the place where we have to turn the corner. This experience often comes after a crisis such as a severe illness, a business disappointment, or the death of a loved one. I "turned the corner" after the sudden death of my husband.

After the funeral, I went home with my daugher, who lives in Switzerland, and stayed several weeks. While there, I went to chapel at the seminary in Ruschlikon. I heard President St. Amant speak on "Turning the Corners in Life." As I sat there, I said to myself, that is what I must do. Yet, I realized I couldn't do it alone.

I had always told others how God could help them in times of trouble. Now I realized the truth of my words. I came back home to stay alone. I faced the vacant chair and the loneliness. Yet, each time as I entered the house, I felt the power of the Holy Spirit reaching out to me.

The words of Isaiah 41:10 spoke to me: "Fear thou not; for I am with thee: be not dismayed; for I am thy God: I will strengthen thee; yea, I will help thee; yea, I will uphold thee with the right hand of my righteousness."

Then, I turned to other Scriptures like these: "For I the Lord thy God will hold thy right hand, saying unto thee, Fear not; I will help thee" (Isa. 41:13). "God is our refuge and strength, a very present help in trouble" (Ps. 46:1).[4]

For this woman, loneliness caused her to turn a corner and renew her faith and thus proved to be a stepping stone to the higher way. Gaining victory over loneliness requires that we give it God's best and our best.

I read somewhere of a man in California who carries on an all-out battle against loneliness. He considers loneliness the world's worst condition and is opposed to loneliness in any form. He wages war against loneliness, attacking it whenever and wherever he finds it, writing letters by the basketful to servicemen, the sick, the shut-in, or to anyone who is lonely. And in doing this wonderful work, he has helped thousands to fight off loneliness.

But the surprising thing about all of this is that the man is a bachelor and lives all alone! He insists, however, that he never feels alone. His life is living proof that living alone does not always make one lonely. Frequently, it is just the opposite.

For example, there are many persons who are *alone* in the midst of bustling cities with thousands of people all around them. Even in the midst of the overcrowded conditions of our day, there are many persons who are, as Edna Ferber said: "As lonesome as a solitary walnut rolling around in a barrel."

You can be lonely in a crowd. Rupert Brooke, the poet, one day in May, 1913, was leaving England for New York. As he looked out over the rail of the ship, he felt terribly lonely for no one had come to see him off. Everyone else seemed to have smiling, waving friends on the dock. He alone was alone.

After a little while, the poet felt he could bear it no longer. And from the deck, catching sight of a dirty little boy all by himself on the pier below, he rushed down the gangway to him, discovered that his name was William and asked, "William, will you wave to me if I give you sixpence?"

"Why, yes," replied the little boy. So the sixpence changed hands, and the poet returned to the ship.

Soon the gangway was lowered, the ropes cast off, and the great liner slowly pulled out into the sea. Some on the pier tried to smile, others unashamedly wept, and all waved handkerchiefs and hats. And a grubby little boy, straining his eyes over the widening water, waved a grubby little hand. And the poet, no longer feeling alone, was comforted. Brooke knew that there were friends in Cambridge and London who were thinking of him as he set sail for the States. But he wanted visible proof, someone on that pier who cared.

One does not have to be a hermit or live like a hermit

to feel alone. Many persons, surrounded by friends and family, put up a brave front; but a feeling of being alone creeps into their hearts and remains there. Oh, they laugh at times and appear to be carefree; but when you sit down with them and talk seriously about life, they drop their guard. The loneliness begins to pour out.

"My laughter is all a front," they admit, "I am very lonely!"

There is but one cure for this kind of loneliness and that is to let Jesus Christ come and dwell with you in your life. His presence is so real to many that they never feel alone.

The owner of a large plantation was taking his daily horseback ride one brisk fall morning. He galloped into a clearing and saw, for the first time, a small shack nestled in the edge of the woods. Pulling on the reins, he came to a stop and noticed an old woman, leaning on a cane, as she stood in the doorway of that tiny dwelling.

Calling to her, he said: "Good morning! Do you live there all alone?"

"No, Sir," was the reply, "Jesus and me—we live here!"

With that blessed arrangement, one is never alone. As the Scriptures remind us: "There is a friend that sticketh closer than a brother" (Prov. 18:24).

But there is still another kind of loneliness. A few years ago a middle-aged man, an average citizen, was appalled by the rapid increase of dives, drug peddling, and racketeering moving into his community, the suburb of a large city. He began a one-man campaign, going into places reputed to be operating illegally, securing evidence of vice and corruption and reporting what he found to the office of the sheriff.

One morning on his way to work, his car was forced to the curb. Three men shoved him into their car and drove off with him. When they reached a distant point out in the country, they tied him, and—with baseball bats—began to beat him, beginning at his feet and slowly pounding him until they reached his head.

The only thing that relieved him of his agony was that he soon became unconscious. Discovered a short while later, he was rushed to a hospital more dead than alive. Suffering from multiple fractures and serious internal injuries, he told a news reporter: "I have fought this thing all alone. No one else seemed to care. Now I am through."

This incident, reported by news services, serves as a reminder of the prophet Elijah who also engaged in what seemed to be a one-man campaign. He challenged the prophets of Baal to a duel and in a demonstration of the power of God, he defeated them.

Following the defeat of the Baal worshipers, the wrath of Queen Jezebel reached out for the prophet, who was forced to run for his life. Seeking a hiding place in the wilderness, Elijah "came to Beersheba in Judah, he left his servant there, while he himself went a day's journey into the desert. He came to a broom tree, sat down under it and prayed that he might die. I have had enough, Lord," he said. "Take my life; I am no better than my ancestors." (1 Kings 19:1-4, NIV).

Note the similarity between the man who crusaded

to clean up his community and Elijah. After being left for dead, he said, "I am through." He felt all alone in his crusade, his campaign for right. No one had offered to help. He stood for right, but he stood alone. This is a dreadful kind of loneliness. But in times like this, we overlook something of tremendous importance. Like Elijah and the crusader, we forget that God is with us.

Elijah was aroused from a nap under the broom tree by an angel, said, "Get up and eat" (1 Kings 19:5, NIV). Bread and water were provided and following another nap, the angel came back a second time to minister to Elijah's needs. Revived by the food and the rest, the prophet traveled forty days and forty nights until he reached Horeb, the mountain of God. He went into a cave there and spent the night. And the word of the Lord came to him, asking: "What are you doing here, Elijah?" (1 Kings 19:9, NIV).

This is a question that could be asked of many a child of man. For just when we think we are going it alone, God ministers to our need, strengthens us as he nourishes us with the Bread of life, lets us rest in him, and then asks: "What are you doing here in your loneliness? What are you doing—feeling sorry for yourself because you feel that you are all alone?" Elijah discovered what many lonely persons must discover: With God by our side we are never alone.

This truth is underlined in a story about Admiral Richard Byrd on one of his first expeditions to the Antarctic region. He planned to stay through the long winter alone, with only radio contact with the camp at Little America. He wanted to make some valuable weather observations while separated from his base by a barrier of ice, cold, and darkness.

Soon the winter closed in, the temperature ranging as low as eighty-five degrees below zero. It was all Byrd could do to keep his blood circulating, even when he was beside the heater he had in his hut. Then, the heater—the very thing that was keeping him from freezing to death—began to give off carbon monoxide gas, and the small gasoline engine that operated his generator also leaked deadly gases.

The famous explorer was seriously poisoned, and believing that he was dying, Byrd prepared final instructions for his men when they would find him in the spring. He wrote what he believed to be farewell letters to his family and then picked up his diary and wrote: "I am not alone!"

God was with him. He felt that wonderful, all-penetrating presence; he was not alone. This explorer, with gifted scientific mind, did not turn to science in his hour of need. Had he done so, he would have said, "I am still alone." But turning to God, he could say—even under overpowering adversity—"I am not alone!"

This truth must be faced: Science often has nothing to say to the deepest levels of human experience. What can science say to a heart being chilled by loneliness? What can science say to a heart broken by grief? What can science do in the face of man's feeling of alienation and isolation from those around him? What can science do when one is required to walk the lonely path of grief?

A pastor recalled an experience in his first church

located in a coal mining community. He said: "My telephone rang at 1 AM and the caller told of a serious accident at one of the mines. I was asked to drive by and pick up an old couple who were linked with our church and bring them quickly to the hospital. Their only son had been crushed by a fall of coal and had but a short time to live."

After arousing the old couple and gently breaking the news, the pastor said: "We hurried to the hospital, entered a ward, and moved toward a bed in the corner. A doctor came out and drew me to one side. 'You are just in time,' he said, 'there is nothing more I can do. You must take over now.' "[5]

There comes the moment when science is mute. There is no healing except from the Balm in Gilead. Beyond science there is God! We look at the Cross on which Christ died. The Son of God come forth from God. In his presence, there is healing for sin, sorrow, and loneliness with his healing touch reaching far beyond Gilead—beyond any modern laboratory where the scientist works.[6]

Our Lord comes to us for the healing of our hearts. Beyond science, there is the God whom we meet in his Son, Jesus Christ, our Lord and Savior. The answer to loneliness is in Christ.

Why do some people feel lonely even in a crowd and others do not feel alone even when they are isolated in an ice hut, cut off from everything and everybody. It can be answered in one word: Christ. He makes the difference.

In describing his devotional life, Foy Valentine, director of the Christian Life Commission of the Southern Baptist Convention, tells how he counteracts the loneliness of hotels and airport waiting rooms. For a quarter of a century his work has required a great deal of travel. Hotels, motels, airplanes, airports, cars, and cabs are not very conducive to the contemplative devotional life.

"But," Valentine says, "look at the Arabian camel. This animal carries a load of five hundred pounds twenty-five miles a day for three days without drinking. Storing water in body tissues, particularly the hump, it draws on these supplies until they can be replenished at some spring in the desert."

Practicing the presence of Christ in his devotional life, Valentine says, "I have evolved a camel-like intake of spiritual water, searching out 'springs in the desert,' oases of devotional time to which I repair for necessary devotional sustenance as I consume whole books of the Bible and drink long and deep at the springs of prayer."

As a kind of general commitment in which his devotional life exists, Valentine keeps a little personal motto with him at all times: "I shall neither withdraw from this world nor be conformed to it." But the early Christian affirmation, the specific commitment in which his devotional life finds its deepest meaning is: "Jesus Christ is Lord!"[7]

Those who walk with Christ are never actually alone. Those who do not walk with Christ are, in a sense, always alone. They are lonely because they lack the essential fellowship with Christ—the companionship which is most necessary to anyone desiring a full and satisfying life.

To those who suffer from loneliness, stifled by the dread feeling that none care for you or that in your efforts to stand up for what is right, you seem to stand alone, let me point you to Christ—one who did walk alone. Of all who have suffered loneliness, his loneliness was the most acute, the most heartbreaking, the most tragic.

In the Scriptures we read: "And Jesus being full of the Holy Ghost returned from Jordan, and was led by the Spirit into the wilderness, Being forty days tempted of the devil" (Luke 4:1-2).

Notice what took place there. For forty days he was tempted of the devil—but not overcome—not the conquered, but the Conqueror. We are told that angels came and ministered unto him, but we are also told of the Spirit ministering unto him, he "returned in the power of the Spirit into Galilee" (Luke 4:14).

Living in the power of the Spirit can also banish loneliness for us and bring us through those solitary trials that sorely vex our souls. A little girl who was fearful of being alone at night in her room had a long talk with an understanding minister. He gave her a verse to say over and over again before she went to sleep: "He shall feed his flock like a shepherd: he shall gather the lambs with his arm, and carry them in his bosom" (Isa. 40:11). She was to think of herself as a lamb kept safely by the Good Shepherd. The idea appealed to her. Soon the nightly fear of being alone in her room went away, replaced by the presence of the loving, caring Shepherd.

Is not this the need of all? To realize that our Lord does not leave us alone in the darkness of this world? He walks with us through the wilderness, yea, even through the fiery furnace and brings us out on the other side. The presence of Christ himself causes us to triumph over loneliness.

And we should receive added strength by remembering that Jesus experienced the most painful loneliness known to man. "Despised and rejected," even the disciples in the darkest hour before and during his crucifixion, forsook him and fled.

And then, came the excruciating loneliness of the Cross. He was taking the penalty for the sins of the world upon his own shoulders. And into the valley of absolute and final rejection he walked in order that we might never have to walk that darksome path.

Through this act of limitless love and devotion, we have the marvelous assurance that Christ will never leave us or forsake us. And that assurance applies to every need.

"I had been deserted and divorced," a woman said, in telling her own sad story. "I had custody of my two children, both little girls. One day as I was working at the kitchen sink, a heavy wave of loneliness came over me, and I began to cry. I cried softly at first, trying to keep my children from seeing it.

"But in a moment I was sobbing and they did see. The six-year-old dragged a chair over to the sink, climbed up on it, and stared into my eyes.

" 'Mother, you're crying,' she said. Then as she climbed down from the chair, she said—in a very matter-of-fact adult way—'Come on. Let's pray about this.' And she sat down at the breakfast table.

"I sat down beside her, and she took my hand in hers with a firm grasp and prayed, 'Dear Lord Jesus, help my mother to be happy. Please don't let her be lonely. Amen.'

"I opened my eyes and looked up. Suddenly the day was radiant. It was full of true joy that had no room for self-pity or loneliness. If I had these two children, nothing else mattered. And I was not alone—not with them and God."[8]

For her, this experience had been a stepping stone to a new and radiant realization of the blessings that were hers. Men and women of faith may take up their lonely vigils in the near and far away outposts of the world, but they are not alone. God is there.

And although at times there may be those who think that they carry on their crusades for right all alone, in reality they are never alone. God also occupies that battlefield and goes against any foe that would harm his children.

Is the way hard for you? Is the loneliness more than you can bear? Remember: Christ Jesus suffered beyond our ability to comprehend, taking the loneliest road of all—the road to the Cross so that none of us might have to utter the despairing cry, "My God, why have you forsaken me?"

And our Lord is always ready to step into the lonely

home and into the lonely heart, ready to drive out the darkness with light.

A poor woman who lived all alone in a small cottage on the outskirts of town was asked if she did not feel the loneliness of the place.

"Oh no," was her reply, "for Faith closes the door at night, and Mercy opens it in the morning."

And so it is for those who live in the loving presence of Christ. As the old hymn says, they are: Never Alone.

> "I've seen the lightning flashing,
> And heard the thunder roll,
> I've felt sin's breakers dashing,
> Trying to conquer my soul;
> I've heard the voice of Jesus,
> Telling me still to fight on,
> He promised never to leave me,
> Never to leave me alone.
> When in affliction's valley
> I'm treading the road of care,
> My Saviour helps me to carry—
> My cross when heavy to bear,
> My feet entangleth with briars,
> Ready to cast me down;
> My Saviour whispered His promise,
> Never to leave me alone.
> No, never alone, . . . No, never alone,
> He promised never to leave me,
> Never to leave me alone."

5

Through the Microscope of Tears

According to the results of a recent scientific survey, doctors report that cheerful people resist disease better than the glum people. In other words, I suppose it could be said that it is the surly bird who always catches the germ. There is no doubt that sorrow and gloom do leave their marks on each of us. If nothing else, it might be anticipated that a colony of germs could be stored up in all the wrinkles that make up a frown.

Now medical research reinforces the truth that the words: "Let a smile be your umbrella" are more than words from an old song—they are also good advice. We now have it on good authority that the shelter of a smile can protect one from the germs, storms, and disturbances of life. In fact, even before the results of the medical research were announced, there were many well-adjusted old-timers who, after years of enduring hard knocks, have learned that a fellow's sense of humor is his bumper which protects him from serious damage in life.

A wonderful old man once appeared on a popular TV program. He received a prize for having won a contest, and he stole the show with his exuberant spirit and quick wit.

"It's easy to see," remarked the admiring master of ceremonies, "that you are one very happy man. What's the secret of being as happy as you are? Let us in on it."

"Why, son," the old man answered, "it's as plain as the nose on your face. When I wake up in the morning, I have two choices. One is to be unhappy; the other is to be happy. And I want you to know, son, that I'm not as dumb as I may look. I'm smart enough to choose happiness."[1]

The happy choice is the wise choice. And yet, sorrow is a very real problem with which we all must deal. Sorrow does not come into our lives by choice, but it comes nonetheless. It is inspiring to observe how well many people seem to deal with life. I am sure that you have known someone whose life was simply radiant: joy beaming out of sparkling eyes; joy bubbling over lips; joy seeming to fairly run from fingertips. You could not come in contact with this person without having a new light come into your life. Some persons are like great electric batteries charged with joy.

If you look into the lives of such radiantly happy persons, you are likely to find that everyone is a man or woman who spends a great deal of time in prayer alone with God.

Recall the Scriptures: "And it came to pass, that, as he was praying in a certain place, when he ceased, one of his disciples said unto him, Lord, teach us to pray, as John also taught his disciples" (Luke 11:1).

The prayer life of Jesus so impressed his disciples that the one thing they asked him to teach them was to pray. As someone has said: "There is no burden of the spirit that is not lightened by kneeling under it." Little by little the bitterest feelings are sweetened by the mention of them in prayer. And agony itself stops swelling and hurting if we can sincerely call upon God in prayer.

The Lord is the source of joy. If we come into contact with him, his infinite joy comes into our lives, giving us joy from within. Despite sorrow and sadness, those who are in fellowship with Christ are satisfied from within.

The men of the world borrow all their joy from without. Joy obtained wholly from without is false, precarious, and of short duration. From without, joy may be gathered but, like gathered flowers, though beautiful for a season, soon withers and dies. But joy from within— stemming from a relationship with our Lord, who came that our joy might be full, has a lasting quality.

A ship, which arrived in New York from Rio de Janeiro, brought a pair of canaries from Rangoon. They were both fine singers, the quality as well as the range of their notes being extraordinary; but the distinguishing characteristic of these songbirds was that they always sang at night.

The Lord has many canaries like that. The distinguishing characteristic of the joyful Christian is that, like Paul and Silas in the prison at Philippi, he is able to sing songs of hope and courage and victory in the darkest night of sorrow. These songs in the night are the most effective testimony the Christian presents as to the joy given to him by his Lord and Savior, Jesus Christ.

The little book of Philippians, written by the apostle

Paul to his beloved friends in the church at Philippi, is literally a song of joy.[2] These four chapters are saturated with joy. Even though the apostle endured the sorrow of imprisonment, being in chains, suffering, hungry and cold, he wrote to his friends at Philippi, saying: "Rejoice in the Lord alway: and again I say, rejoice" (Phil. 4:4).

Philippians 4:11 is one of my favorite verses: "I have learned, in whatsoever state I am, therewith to be content." This is the key in dealing with sorrow and sadness and hardship. It points out the truth that circumstances do not determine joy. We determine our joy by how we react to the circumstances. Joy is not dependent upon external physical circumstances. Joy is not dependent upon the fluctuation of material things that come and go. These things are not essential to joy itself. Paul was saying, "I have learned to be content in whatever state I am, whatever the circumstances might be, I have learned contentment."

This is possible, the apostle Paul would have us know, not because of his power—but because of God's power. God is able to turn sorrow into joy because of the power that he brings into our lives. This is amplified in Philippians 4:19: "But my God shall supply all your need according to his riches in glory by Christ Jesus." The source of power is in God himself.[3]

The psalmist said: "He hath put a new song in my mouth" (Ps. 40:3). This is a cheering, heartening word that interests everyone. It is a word that is needed in every age, and it is especially needed by the jaded generation of which we are a part. Life has grown old and stale for many persons. Instead of finding new songs, they have found old yawns.

But here the psalmist had discovered a new song. He had a story to tell that we need to hear. The source of this new song flows from the fountain of inspiration. This song is not a child of chance. It is not a creature of circumstance. It is not a song of youth, for sometimes youth sings, but sometimes it does not. To some young people life seems sad and drab; they seem to be weary, listless souls. So youth is not the source for the inspiration of this song on the lips of the psalmist. Also, this song does not have its rise in the hills of prosperity and success. There is no hint in the verse that the psalmist had found either fame or fortune.

What is the source of this new song? God. "He hath put a new song in my mouth," the psalmist declared joyously. This song is born of the inexhaustible resources that are locked in the heart of God. "My God shall supply all your needs according to his riches and glory by Christ Jesus" (Phil. 4:19). Then, too, the psalmist's song is a song of deliverance. "He brought me up also out of an horrible pit, out of the miry clay" (Ps. 40:2).

I read somewhere the story of a man caught in quicksand. One moment this man was walking in safety. Then suddenly his path began to cling to his feet a bit. A few more steps and he was bogged down to his knees.

He then began to struggle frantically. But the more he struggled, the deeper he sank. Soon the treacherous sand had reached his waist. By this time, the unfortunate victim had become desperate—he realized he was being swallowed up in this pit. He cried for help, but there was no response. At last, the sand swallowed him and the struggle was over.

The psalmist was once like this man. He, too, was sinking and was sure that all was over—he cried desperately for help. And the loving God answered his cry.[4] He reached out a helpless hand and that hand was seized by One who was mighty, and he felt himself lifted to safety. From that time on, he had a song upon his lips, a song of deliverance. Some of us can join in the singing of this song, for such a song fits every man who has been lifted out of the pit of life by a loving God.

The song of the psalmist is a song of security, in spite of the sorrow that comes to each of us in our day-by-day existence. "He set my feet upon a rock, and established my goings" (Ps. 40:2). Knowing this, one can walk today with an assured confidence. His confidence is not born of his faith in himself but of his faith in God. The Lord makes it possible for us to sing with the psalmist, "Yea, though I walk through the valley of the shadow of death, I will fear no evil" (Ps. 23:4).

That one, who has the truth of this psalm in his heart, has footing for the road of life that is firm and secure. He does not look to tomorrow with feverish fear. The old horror is gone, and he can now look ahead—knowing that the God who keeps him today will be more than sufficient for him tomorrow. This feeling is similar to the relieved feeling experienced by the nervous driver as he approaches an extremely narrow pass on a torturous road in the Rocky Mountains, only to be confronted by the following reassuring highway sign:

"Oh, yes, you can. Millions have!"

Sometimes we cannot help but think: *Nobody has ever been as badly off as I am now.* And when we brood over our problems, our sorrows enlarge themselves until they obscure our entire horizon. Yet, if we think of some of the things others have had to suffer, and especially if we remember the unfailing grace of God, our problems become easier to bear. We realize that it is a part of our human situation to undergo sorrow.

At the same time, we must remember the reassurance of Exodus 15:2: "The Lord is my strength and song, and he is become my salvation." It was easy for Moses and the people of Israel to sing this song. The Lord had won, and they were on his side. But it also applies in time of loss and defeat.

Robert E. Goodrich, Jr., has a sermon entitled "Mourning Becomes You." In it he tells the story of Governor and Mrs. Lawrence of Pennsylvania who, in a tragic highway accident, lost two teenage sons. At first, they were senseless with grief. They wondered if their grieving would ever end. Then one day they wrote a letter of sympathy to parents, total strangers, who had experienced a similar loss. Then another letter was written, then another.

Soon they began to discover a purpose in their mourning and a comfort in their ministry to others within this fellowship of sorrow. There is great strength to be gained in the fellowship of sorrow if it is within the circle of faith.

The Toccoa Falls, Georgia, tragedy verifies this fact. Students and faculty members of small Toccoa Falls Bible College will tell you that it is faith in the Lord that has sustained them since thirty-nine persons were killed in a flood after a dam broke on November 6, 1977. The dam broke in the dead of night after heavy rain, washing down from the lake, atop a waterfall, and engulfing dormitories and mobile homes where students and faculty members slept. Experts have studied the survivors of the dam failure and flood in an effort to understand the psychological reactions of those who have lived through similar disasters in other sections of our nation.

The studies have shown that the people at Toccoa Falls came out very well and were in better mental health than other communities where the personal loss was not nearly as great. The adjustment by those who lost loved ones and fellow students is attributed to faith in God. Strong commitment to God gave them an understanding and a strength for what had happened to them—a strength which people in other flood-wrecked communities in the nation did not have.[5]

The tragedy was shattering to many, but the bright spot in it all was that the faith of those who survived had given them a new song in the face of sorrow. This kind of song is a benediction to those who possess it. For song means joy and gladness and our present-day religion seems to be a bit short of true joy.

A recent survey indicates that the typical church member wants his minister to be a happy person. The survey shows that churchgoers do not take to the minister who always looks as if he has just counted his sparse, Sunday evening crowd. For many a preacher, the only thing longer than his sermon is his face, and that is no compliment.

All of which is a reminder of the incident concerning the man who was sent to a railroad station to meet a visiting minister. He had never seen the preacher before, so as the train came to a stop and passengers filed off, he watched closely and tried to select from the crowd a face which he considered appropriate to the clergy.

Approaching a gentleman with a particularly sour face, he said, "Excuse me, Sir, are you a minister?"

"No," was the answer, "I just look this way because I have stomach trouble."

Ministers need to remember to practice and reflect the joy of the Lord. All would do well to remember that "the joy of the Lord is your strength" (Neh. 8:10).

A faith that is short of joy is also short of strength, for joy is a source of strength in our hours of bereavement. It is a source of strength when our dreams fail to come true. It is a steady staff upon which to lean when the rain is on the roof and the light has gone out of the skies.

It was so in the case of the woman who wrote just before she died, "The cancer has spread to my liver and there is not much hope. I shall hate to leave my family." But you can sing a new song because Jesus lives and because of her faith, so does she. Actually, she lives more than she ever lived before.[6]

Then there is the new song of hope for parents whose children are living outside of God's will and thus causing their parents pain. This is hard to bear, but in Christ there is hope that even this sorrow shall turn to joy. This sorrow, when viewed from the perspective of faith, can prove to be a stepping stone to the higher way. There can be a new song for every person who looks not to his sorrows but to Christ. There can be the song of joy because Jesus is Lord, Lord of hope, and in him we shall yet have everlasting joy.

As a pastor, one of the saddest experiences of my ministry came one afternoon. An abrupt phone call brought the almost unbelievable news that a twelve-year-old girl in my church had collapsed during a physical education exercise at school with a cerebral hemorrhage. She had been rushed to the hospital, put under intensive care, but there were no signs of life. The hemorrhage had been so massive that she was now being kept alive only with the aid of machines and artificial respiration. There was a sorrow that seemed too hard to believe.

When I arrived at the hospital, the parents were pacing up and down the hospital corridor. We went into the small chapel; I talked to the mother, and we prayed together. We found it hard to believe that this fine, apparently healthy young girl could go off to school shortly after eight o'clock and by mid-afternoon be in a hospital intensive care unit more dead than alive. The doctors and nurses worked frantically, but there was no hope. All signs of life were gone, and the doctor came in and gave that last terrible verdict to the mother. They had done all that they could do, the doctor said, but it had not been enough.

The body of the little girl was removed to the funeral home and services planned for two days later. The next afternoon when her small six-year-old sister came home from school, I went out to see her with the hope that we might have a chance to talk. You could tell that the little girl found it hard to understand, hard to believe, hard to take in. Death had come so quickly, and the sister on whom she had depended was gone.

I talked to the mother and the daughter, led them in prayer, and left. When I reached the driver's side of my automobile and started to open the door, I turned around to see the little sister standing behind me. She looked up and said, "When you see God, would you give him this for Lisa."

I reached down and took the note printed on a small piece of paper, opened it and read: "LISA, I LOVE YOU." I swallowed a couple of large lumps in my throat and said, "I will be talking to God today, and I will tell him to give the message to Lisa."

She ran back to the house, satisfied that the message would be delivered. And as I drove away, brushing a tear from my cheek, I knew once again that love can banish sorrow and can wipe away tears. Even the sorrow of death and the loss of a loved one can be banished by love.

A reality of life is that tears will come as a result of death. We have all passed through that experience at sometime, in some way. Tears will be shed. But we can be thankful that beyond all this, there is a land to which we are going, through Jesus Christ, our blessed Lord, a land where there are no tears. For in the book of Revelation, where John saw the movements of heaven, he declared: "God shall wipe away all tears from their eyes" (Rev. 7:17).

Toward this tearless land we are journeying. The sorrow which we now endure is but a stepping stone to bring us closer to the land where there are no tears, where we will have no sorrow. But whether the distance is short or long, we are all headed for that tearless land if we are in Christ Jesus, our Lord.

Someday we are going to come to the place where there will be no disappointments of friendship, no blasted hopes, no shattered health; where there will be no more aches and pains, no more death, no more sorrow. It will be a place where we will bask together in the light of the eternal sun. And more than anything else, this realization gives us strength for the living of today, as we look through the microscope of tears toward a brighter tomorrow.

Jon Appleton, a fellow minister in Athens, Georgia, told of an experience he had while serving as volunteer chaplain of the week at a local hospital. On Monday, his first day of service, he had an emergency call from one of the nurses concerning a woman who was in critical condition following childbirth. The child was still-born.

Arriving at the hospital, he found the family gathered

in a circle with the father, tears streaming down his face, lifting a fervent prayer to God. In the circle with the father were four of his five children (the youngest child was with a neighbor) and his mother-in-law. The scene was quiet and heart-touching.

Appleton said, "I was awed by the quietness, by the weeping, by the energy of petition; and, when I was invited into the circle, I felt a peace in the midst of the storm." Of course, time and the blessings and presence of God along with the miracles of medical attention would verify the mother's condition. But at that moment that wife and mother was blessed in her struggle by the love of a family who prayed, "God—whatever is best for Mama, give to us the strength of love and understanding." While life was going on routinely for many persons around our city on that day, this struggle to live was being inacted in a hospital corridor.

Sooner or later, all of us are confronted with the extremes in life—sorrow, life, death. Many have found their strength by uniting to say in prayer, "Whatever is best—give to us the strength of love and understanding." This is using sorrow as a stepping stone to greater submission to the will of God.

One day I was driving past some small business establishments on the edge of town. I was fascinated by a sign, hanging over a welding shop, which read: "We Mend Everything Except a Broken Heart and the Break of Day." Not discounting this man's attempt to advertise his skill as a welder, you must admit that he does present a truth to be considered. The truth is this:

Inevitably, each man must bear his own burden and shed his own tears. As John Donne once said, "Never send to know for whom the bell tolls; it tolls for thee."

The cruelest advice is often the injunction, used by certain well-meaning persons, "Don't cry." Often it is better that the tears flow and the grief run its normal course than to be bottled up inside. Some of the greatest lessons of life come through sorrow. Indeed, sorrow can mean a clearer view of life through the microscope of tears. As the old saying has it: "He that lacks time to mourn, lacks time to mend." A cloudless day never produced a rainbow. It shares its bright hues only with those who first endure the storm.

Duke K. McCall was talking by long distance phone with his brother when the surgeon came into the hospital room to report on his sister-in-law. His brother returned to the phone and said, with a breaking voice, "Bad news—cancer." On hearing the news, McCall says he caught a plane home, as soon as he could so he could visit his sister-in-law in the hospital.

All during the flight he turned the situation over in his mind. He asked himself again and again the question: *How do you tell a beautiful, young woman that heaven is closer—and make it good news?*

That was what was on his mind as he entered the hospital room. But she had already prepared a message for her visitors. It was a little sign in front of the flowers on the window sill beyond her bed. It said, simply but completely: "God is greater than all my problems."

This is using sorrow as a stepping stone to the higher way. With this kind of faith, sorrow can present a clearer view of life through the miscroscope of tears. And the view is plainly this: God is sufficient for all of our sorrows and greater than all of our problems.

6
Running with Patience

The young woman who sat in the pastor's study was only a few days past her eighteenth birthday. She tried to appear calm, but the fidgeting of her hands and the nervous act of flipping at her hair gave her away. The awkward silence underlined the seriousness of her problem.

It was a long time before she managed to speak. Then there was one word, a second word, and another: "We . . . couldn't . . . wait," she said. "I'm pregnant. We had to get married, and we did get married—but it only lasted two months."

Perhaps of all the words spoken, three words that can prove to be most damaging are: "We couldn't wait." Patience is a rare quality seldom found in the lives of those who are called upon to live in this frantic day. But patience—that willingness to wait—can be a stepping stone to a more satisfying life.

The problem is that so many are by nature impatient, and others respond with impatience to the irritations and frustrations that abound today. "Keep your cool" is a pet phrase with the youth and when you think about it, this is important for young and old. A tourist guide in South America, commenting on the height of a jagged volcanic mountain, said: "This would have been our tallest mountain if it hadn't blown its top."

So it is with many persons: they diminish themselves by blowing their tops. This bit of verse offers excellent advice:

> A wise old owl lived in an oak;
> The more he saw, the less he spoke.
> The less he spoke, the more he heard—
> Why can't we all be like that bird?

It is a good question and the wisdom of it is fortified by the fact that God gave us two eyes, two ears, and only one tongue.

A good definition of an angry man is this: He is one who opens his mouth and shuts his eyes. In a blind fit of temper, he closes his eyes to all that he should see, failing to get a clear picture of the situation, while leaving his mouth open to do the damage.

Since the beginning of time, the same tragic story has been repeated. People have destroyed themselves and others with fits of anger. Alexander the Great was known as *the Great* because of his world conquests. But one night during a celebration with his top ranking generals, a lifelong friend of Alexander, General Clitus, reminded Alexander that the conqueror's father, Philip, was also a truly great man and might have met with the same success if he had only received the cooperation given to Alexander.

In a jealous rage, Alexander lost his patience, unleashed his temper, and reached for his sword. A wise attendant noticing the flush of anger on the king's face, had removed the weapon. The general was told to leave, but Clitus had now become angry so he slipped back into the hall and concealed himself behind the draperies that lined the wall.

In a moment of silence he tossed out insults intended for Alexander who grabbed the spear of a guard, and lunged it through the drapes into the heart of his friend. As General Clitus slumped before him, gasping his last breath, Alexander was immediately grief-stricken, but it was too late. The ghastly deed was done and all the tears and sleepless nights to follow could not erase the sight of his friend on the floor in a pool of blood. The emperor who could conquer the world was in turn conquered by his own anger and impatience.

Anger is destructive and is a conqueror—a conqueror of the great and the small, the big and the little, the poor and the rich. However, we would do well to understand that there is a constructive, as well as a destructive, kind of anger. We often refer to justified anger as righteous indignation which can be used as a stepping stone to right wrongs and battle evil. This is an anger that disappears as quickly as the cause is corrected.

With righteous indignation, Jesus denounced hypocrisy and injustice and drove out of the Temple those who defiled this sacred place of prayer. His indignation, justified by the circumstances, was used for setting right that which was wrong.

In Ephesians, we find the key: "Be angry"; but the

warning follows immediately: "Do not sin!" (4:26). And further good advice is given: "Do not let the sun go down on your wrath" (author's translation).

The failing of most is at the point of destructive anger where all patience is lost, tempers flare, and injurious wrath is carried over into another day of conflict. We may offer many excuses for losing our patience, but the common reason is inner tension that gets beyond control, causing us to boil and burn inside until—like a boiler with too much steam—we blow up, damaging whatever happens to be in the way.

The problem is as old as man. Look at Cain and Abel. Cain lost his patience and became angry with his brother. He struck him and killed him. Moses listened to the murmurings of the children of Israel, hearing their complaints that they would rather be slaves in Egypt than proceed through the wilderness, until his patience was exhausted. When God told him to speak to the rock to bring forth a spring of water, Moses disobeyed. Lifting his rod high above his head, he struck the rock twice. Forty years later, Moses found himself on the edge of the Promised Land, able to look over Jordan but told by God that he could not enter. Uncontrolled anger deprives us of the greatest satisfactions of life.

And there is but one wise response: We must match spiritual power against the burden of anger that pushes us down and prevents us from living the calm and assured life. We must seek God's guidance and help in keeping a tight rein on our anger. If an angry man is one who closes his eyes and opens his mouth, then the love of God can change all that. The God of love is able to close mouths and open eyes and hearts to the kind of peace that only he can bring to every strained situation.

Exercising patience is a giant step that contributes to our growing larger as a person and as a servant of God. But this is not an easy step. We are an impatient nation, an impatient people. We have instant coffee and instant mashed potatoes, but that is not enough. Whatever it is, we want it instantly. Patience has gone out of style.

Sometime ago I stood on Madison Avenue in New York City watching the people hurry by. An elderly lady, who identified herself as being from England, also stood nearby and viewed the passing parade of hurrying humanity.

"Where are they all going?" she asked.

"I don't know," I replied, "but they are in a hurry to get there!"

Those people were living proof that patience has gone out of style. *Impatience* is the word nowadays. Everything is fast, and we want it faster. It is a commentary on our day that many persons are so harried and hurried they do not wait on the Lord or take time to listen to the voice of God. The result is great personal loss.

While on an automobile trip through Georgia, a man from the city met a local character who spent most of his time on the porch of a crossroads general store. His slowness of speech, deliberate actions, and calm philosophy of life prompted the gentleman from the city to ask him about these obvious characteristics.

"Well, Son," he drawled, "it don't pay nobody to be in a hurry. You just always pass up more than you catch up with."

He had a point there, a point which many overlook as they rush along. Failing to wait upon the Lord, one is apt to pass up the genuine values of life as he chases after the trivial. Admittedly, patience is not a popular virtue today. Personal comfort has been cultivated among us at the expense of patience. We rebel at a moment's delay over anything which does not go our way.

Advertisements for new automobiles emphasize the ease and comfort features, including deep pile carpets, soft cushions and upholstering, plus special power options to assure effortless driving. In fact, they have everything in the new automobile to soothe the impatient man except a gadget to fit over the mouth of the backseat driver. Everything is designed to make us more comfortable, to save us from the slightest irritation. But this kind of shallow, superficial living has caused some to merely look on the surface of life and live on the surface of life. The modern malady is not taking root—not being planted here or there.

As you ride over the countryside, you will notice trees that have blown down because they had too many branches above ground and not enough strong rootage below ground. It is easy to observe the same failing among people. Lives have broken down because of too much stress and strain, not enough spiritual staunchness; too much hurry and not enough taking time to be holy; too much superficiality and not enough deep spirituality; too much impatience with life and not enough patience in the Lord.

Someone has defined patience as willingness to adjust our effort to God's time element. Patience is that wonderful virtue which enables us to want God's will to be done, and not our will to be done. Hebrews 12:1 offers excellent advice at this juncture: "Let us lay aside every weight, and the sin which doth so easily beset us and let us run with patience the race that is set before us."

Selfishness—which causes us to be impatient, to want everything our way and not God's way—is a burdensome weight that should be set aside.

Job, that indomitable character in the Old Testament, had to put aside the weight of selfishness before he could display his marvelous attribute of patience. You recall that Job was mocked and criticized by his friends. He was reduced to sitting in a pile of ashes, scraping the sores which covered his body with a piece of broken pottery. Still, with a glowing display of faith and humble forgetfulness of self, Job emerged triumphant from the depths of despair.

There is one other thing we should consider before we leave the physical suffering of Job. The greatest patience is not always that which is required under physical trials. The severest test of our patience could be that which is called for when we are provoked by our fellowman. The worst suffering may not be bodily

pain but the pain from the heartbreaking hurts which
loved ones send our way.

The truth is, there are a number of persons who were
born in the objective case and the kickitive mood.
There is no other way to explain them. No matter what
you do, you simply cannot please them.

One morning a loving wife turned to her hard-to-
please husband and asked, "Darling, what would you
like for breakfast?"

Scowling, her husband barked out his reply: "Coffee
and toast, grits and sausage, and two eggs—one scram-
bled and one fried!"

His wife was determined to go to any length to
please him. So she applied all of the skills at her command to prepare a perfect breakfast for her husband.
When he sat down at the table, she waited patiently,
hoping for some small word of praise. Instead, after a
quick glance, he snorted: "Well, I'll be—if you didn't go
and scramble the wrong egg!"

It would seem that some have no other object in life
except to object to everything. They fail to realize how
objectionable they are in their objections. Long-suffer-
ing patience is a must for those who live in a tense
environment with the chronic complainer. Achieve-
ments of space exploration not withstanding, let us be
reminded that before man learns to control outer
space, he needs to learn to control the inner space that
lies immediately under his hat. While seeking to control
guided missiles in outer space, man, in his impatience,
has not yet learned how to control himself. After all,

what good are guided missiles so long as we have mis-
guided lives?

From the world of sports, news agencies recorded an
unusual incident in the Rose Bowl game of 1929, between the University of California and Georgia Tech.
California center, Roy Riegels, received a fumble on
Tech's thirty-three yard line and ran toward the wrong
goal, seventy yards away.

One of his own teammates finally tackled him on the
one-foot line. As Riegels realized his awful mistake, an
agonized expression spread over his face, but the run
was over and the outcome of the game decided. California's attempt to kick from behind the goal was
blocked and Tech scored a safety which brought victory.

In our contemporary life there are many persons
repeating the mistake of Riegels: They are running in
the wrong direction. This is a far more serious mistake
which can result in losing more than a football game. It
can result in losing the game of life. A sense of urgency
throbs from the question: Are you frantically running in
the wrong direction?

"Let us run with patience the race that is set before
us" (Heb. 12:1), the Scriptures warn. And how we need
to learn this patience, to cultivate this kind of patience—not only in the larger, more complicated issues
but also in the little daily annoyances that dog our trail.

One morning at a crowded intersection a car stalled,
holding up a long line of other vehicles behind it. Obviously flustered, the man driving the car got out, lifted

the hood of the car to investigate. As he did, the driver of the car behind him began honking his horn. The noise continued without letup until the driver of the stalled car, unable to discover the trouble, suddenly straightened up and spoke to the impatient motorist behind him: "If you'll fix my car," he said calmly, "I'll be glad to come back there and keep blowing your horn for you."

In our impatience we sometimes think that mere noise will make a bad situation right, whether it be by sitting on the horn or yelling. Actually, a display of uncontrolled temper rarely accomplishes anything— although there are some who keep on exploding nonetheless.

It is difficult to turn a high temper to good use, but you have to admire the resourcefulness of the wife whose husband became enraged at tripping over a loose carpet on the living room floor. "If you don't do something about it," he shouted, "I'm going to lose my temper with that rug!"

With a smile, the wife said: "I don't blame you, dear, and if I were you, I would take that rug out in the yard, throw it over the clothesline, get me a big stick, and give it a good beating."

Such good results, however, are rarely accomplished. For it seems that intelligent people, able to manage large enterprises and make important corporate decisions, are frequently blind to the fact that patience and an even temper are stepping stones that get us a great deal farther along life's road. There are frenzied people who continue to fume and fret their way through life—losing their cool and blowing their tops at the slightest provocation. A woman who had suddenly come into a large sum of money went to Alaska to look over a fox farm. Friends had told her of the fabulous profits to be made in such a venture. After admiring a beautiful silver fox specimen, she asked a guide: "Just how many times can a fox be skinned for his fur?"

At first, the guide thought she was kidding, but seeing that the woman was serious, he answered: "Well, Lady, after three or four times, the little rascal kind of begins to lose his temper."

If the testimony of the guide is accepted, then it must be agreed that many of us are more unruly than the average fox. For it doesn't take a "skinning"—it takes only a little abrasion, the slightest irritation of the skin of pride, to send us off on a violent tantrum.

How many times we display our impatience toward the driver of the car in front of us who, according to our evaluation, is too dumb to own a driver's license. And a new dictionary would have to be written to include all the words muttered about the hapless motorist caught napping when the red light suddenly changes to green.

As we view humanity's wearisome scene, we must not look through the eyes of scorn but must observe man's failings and frailties through the patient eyes of love. Too often we do not look closely enough at the situation of our fellowman before losing our patience.

A professor in Scotland once called upon a student to stand in class and read. "Hold your book in the other hand," the professor said.

Apparently paying no attention to the command, the student went on reading. "Do you hear me, Sir?" the professor exclaimed, "I said, hold your book in the other hand!"

The student stopped reading, still holding the book as before, but now having his head cast down.

"Sir!" shouted the professor. Then the student slowly raised his other arm—from which the hand had been cut off.

We must take a closer look at our fellowman; indeed, we must take the deep and holy view of all persons, looking upon them with more patience and love. Many have been severely wounded by life. Understanding, love, and patience can be soothing balm for the hurts of mankind.

There may be days when you say, "I want to be patient. I really do. My feet just can't seem to get a grip on the stepping stone of patience. I want to be patient with everyone, but sometimes I just can't stand it!" But you can. You can stand it because our Lord will stand with you.

The writer of Hebrews 12:1, recognizing God's power to change us and meet every need, told us how it was to be done: "Let us lay aside every weight"—the weight of selfishness and shortsightedness—"the sin which doth so easily beset us, and let us run with patience the race that is set before us."

7

When Life Puts You Down, Faith Pulls You Up

All the water in the world will not sink a ship unless the water gets inside the ship. Equally true is the fact that all of the disappointing circumstances will not sink a life if one refuses to allow discouragement to get inside and dominate life. We have all known persons disappointed in their families, their work, their friends, and even in their health. Still, they were not discouraged.

In contrast, others seem to live a charmed life. Everything appears to go their way. They have wonderful health. Their children do well. Friends remain loyal. They grow wealthier each day as their businesses prosper. And yet, strangely enough, they suffer from discouragement.[1] Why is this? It is because, more often than not, we surrender to the flood of discouragement and sink our own ships or make our own sink holes.

One time a motorist, bogged down in a muddy road, paid a passing farmer ten dollars to pull the stuck automobile out with his tractor. When he was back on dry ground and ready to continue his journey down the road, the motorist said to the farmer: "Man, you charged me ten bucks! At those prices I would think you would be pulling people out of the mud night and day."

"No, I can't do that," replied the farmer. "At night, I am busy hauling water to pour in the mud hole in the road."

There is truth here worth noting. When we get bogged down, many of the holes we get ourselves into don't just happen. They are constructed on purpose and are often of our own doing.

However, we can be grateful that the tractors of faith, courage, perseverance, and determination have pulled many out of what seemed to be hopeless situations. Even when bogged down in a mess of your own making, faith can lift you up and out. But you must first step on the steady stone of faith.

In this way, when confronting numerous daily problems, we have a dynamic that enables us to cope. As life's burdens drag you down, faith raises you up. I do not know of any word more desperately needed in modern life than this word of *hope*. It is a word that points us to God in all the disappointments of life—a word of rescue that keeps life from sinking. The wise have learned from the past that how you react to the experiences of life is as significant as the experiences themselves. Harry N. Holmes of Australia used to say, "Life is what you make it and how you take it."[2]

Our experiences are the raw materials we use to shape life. If we look at the dark side of our experiences and live in the shadows of our anxieties, we will find life a dreary, discouraging struggle. But God is continually calling us to lift up our hearts and live in the light of his presence and strength rather than in the darkness of discouragement.

Discouragement is injurious to your health. Dr. Charles Mayo of the world-famous Mayo Clinic said: "Worry affects the circulation, the heart, the glands, the whole nervous system. I have never known a man who died from overwork, but many who died of worry."[3]

Since life seems to come with built-in difficulties, the emphasis must be placed not on what life deals you but on how you react to what life brings. To support this premise, observe the similarity between the game of football and the game of life: Both endeavors have their setbacks, and it is not unusual in one's daily existence to be thrown for a loss. But the hard-nosed competitor knows that the victory belongs to those who say, "When the going gets tough, the tough get going." Like the team on the gridiron, the individual who wins in life's arena is the one who never gives into discouragement.

Young people frequently inspire us with their tenacity. In the dictionary of some young persons, there is no such word as *fail*. Note the incident concerning the boy who wanted to march in the circus parade. When the circus came to town, the word was passed that the bandmaster needed a trombonist, so the boy quickly volunteered. As it turned out, the young man had not marched a block before the dreadful noises from his horn caused two elderly ladies to faint and a horse to run away.

Demanding an explanation, the bandmaster shouted, "Why didn't you tell me you couldn't play the trombone?"

The boy said, "How did I know? I never tried before!" This determined, positive stance represents the attitude needed by all.

Acts 13:15 says: "Men and brethren, if you have any message of encouragement for the people, by all means speak" (Phillips).

These words were spoken in Asia Minor to Paul and Barnabas who entered the temple that morning to worship. They were itinerant preachers, traveling from place to place interpreting the Scriptures. The presiding elder of the synagogue read from the Law and the Prophets, and then looking toward the strange men in their midst, invited them to speak if they had any word of encouragement for the people. If they had come to boast or argue or complain; if they had an axe to grind, they were out of place. That being their intention, they could go out and hire a hall or rent an auditorium. But if they had a word of encouragement for people with anxieties, uncertainties, and burdens, they were invited to speak that heartening word. Without a moment's hesitation, these men of God responded. There followed such a glorious service, they were implored to return the next week and repeat the same words. For the Word of God in its fullness is a cheerful word—a word that is cheering and encouraging for the souls of men.

In the face of a world full of upsetting problems, this would seem to be the condition of any helpful message: encouragement. Hear the glad tidings: The first word of Paul and Barnabas and the first word of the gospel is that God has fulfilled his promises in his Son Jesus. Other words of encouragement flow from this great word, including hope for men and nations; hope for a world that is peaceful, decent, and loving. This is not to ignore the powers of darkness that are awesome in their might and seeming success. But with the sure knowledge that God is to have the final victory, we must not fall victim to discouragement.

Once upon a time Satan announced that he was offering his inventions, devices, and tools for sale to anyone who would pay the price. On the day of the sale the tools were all displayed: malice, hatred, jealousy, selfishness, deceit, and all of the other instruments of evil were marked with a price.

Apart from the rest, lay a plain wedge-shaped tool, much worn, and priced much higher than any of the others. Someone asked Satan what it was.

"Oh, that tool—that is discouragement," answered Satan.

"Why have you priced such a simple tool so high?" the questioner continued.

"Because," Satan replied, "it is the most valuable tool I have. You see, I can reach a man with discouragement when I cannot get near him with any of my other devices. And once I have him discouraged, I can use him in whatever way I want," Satan concluded.

And so it came to pass that Satan's price for discouragement was so high that it was never sold. Satan still owns it and uses it, and it remains to this day his most valuable tool.

Discouragement always waits in the wings, ready and anxious to attack. Often well-intentioned persons allow themselves to be used as means of discouraging those around them who are giving their very best to life's tasks.

Take the case of Thomas A. Edison. Totally dedicated to the invention of the electric light, he tirelessly toiled in his laboratory until one night, after many experiments had failed, the breakthrough came: Wires were connected and the bulb glowed brightly! Eureka! Success! Suddenly, Edison heard his wife's voice: "For goodness sake, Tom, it's 2 AM. Turn out that light and come to bed!"

It reminds you of the attitude of all disgruntled, discouraging souls who seem to delight in taking the fire out of everything one tries to do. You know the ones: They hold the "World Olympic championship" in throwing cold water.

If enthusiasm is contagious, some people have been rendered immune by having a pin stuck into every exciting idea that comes along. Where one person is enjoying the warmth of enthusiasm, there is usually someone around to turn down the thermostat. But the world would be a brighter, happier place if we had more persons eager to turn up the light—not turn out the light—of enthusiasm and encouragement.

In spite of all who shout gloom and doom, there is no real reason for despair. Ponder these questions: Where is your God? Where is your hope now? Well, God is where he has always been and our hope is in Christ. We must believe that we or our children or our children's children shall yet see "the goodness of the Lord in the land of the living" (Ps. 27:13). Why can we believe that? Because we have seen God in Jesus

Christ, and there is a word of hope for mankind.

Furthermore, there is another word of encouragement, a direct and personal word, for everyone of us
wherever we are and in whatever condition we stand.
This is the word: God is not far from any of us, "for in
him we live, and move, and have our being" (Acts
17:28).

How near is he? Nearer than breathing, closer than
hands or feet. In our toil and in our leisure, in our joy
and in our pain, in our waking and in our slumber, God
is with us. He gives us light, not light on the distant
scene, not light for next year, next week, or tomorrow
but light for today. So let us take courage—not in ourselves—but in God's power. His strength enables us to
stay with the plow and continue the journey.

A businessman is said to have a large picture in his
office of a cat hanging on the limb of a tree with its fore-
paws hooked over the bark, struggling to stay in that
tree. Printed at the bottom of the picture are the words:
"Hang in there, Baby!"[4] This could be interpreted by
some as a near description of their situation. They feel
that they are just barely hanging on. And although it
might be intended as a bracing word by well-meaning
friends, a great deal more is required than the rather
frivolous directive: "Hang in there!"

Undergirding power is needed to sustain and hold
up life and this means no less than the power of the living Lord. Without this kind of support, man cannot
maintain his grip on life. The tree of discouragement
has slippery bark. This is why, in his moment of deepest
despair, when neither wind, earthquake, nor fire could

uphold him, Elijah was supported by the still, small voice of God. And thus, the Spirit speaks wisely through the psalmist to us and to all discouraged Elijahs: "Be still, and know that I am God" (Ps. 46:10).

In making a profound observation, the canny Scotsman, Thomas Carlyle was sharing a splendid truth when he said: "Man lives by believing in something."[5]

Faith and courage constitute two of our most basic needs. But contrary to the thinking of some, faith is more than a storm cellar to which men can run for shelter from the storms of life. Faith is an inner power which provides the strength to endure those storms and their consequences with serenity.

In times of sore distress, faith has the miraculous capacity to boost ordinary men and women to greatness. Courage is born of faith, and if we overcome the fears which beset us, we must have courage. Let us understand that courage falls into two categories: physical courage which equips one to brave physical dangers, and moral courage which empowers one to shoulder the burdens and take the heavy blows of life without losing heart.[6] Above all, courage results from having faith in ourselves, faith in the righteousness of our cause and more importantly faith in the promises of God. The Lord does help those who help themselves. We do our part and God does his.

A widow had six children and, astonishingly enough, adopted twelve more. She did such a stupendous job of raising, supporting, and training them that she won public recognition for this outstanding achievement.

A newspaper reporter, sent out to interview her, asked, "How did you ever handle such a gigantic task and not worry about it?"

"Oh," she replied, "I entered into a partnership."

"A partnership?" queried the reporter.

"Yes," the widow came back, "some years ago I entered a partnership with God. I made a deal with him. I said I would do the work if he would do the worrying. And ever since that time, I have not had one hour of worry."

This kind of partnership with God eliminates worry and discouragement. The apostle Paul had entered just such a partnership with his Lord, and the strength of this divine merger enabled this determined Christian warrior to ask:

Who shall separate us from the love of Christ? shall tribulation, or distress, or persecution, or famine, or nakedness, or peril, or sword? Nay, in all these things we are more than conquerors through him that loved us. For I am persuaded, that neither death, nor life, nor angels, nor principalities, nor powers, nor things present, nor things to come, Nor height, nor depth, nor any other creature, shall be able to separate us from the love of God, which is in Christ Jesus our Lord (Rom. 8:35,37-39).

"Well," you chime in, "that was easy enough for Paul to say. He had a wonderful conversion; he was well-born and well-bred; he had a fine education and Roman citizenship, even though he was a Jew in a conquered land. Small wonder Paul felt that way." But wait a moment. Are you forgetting exactly what he wrote to the Corinthians about his own life? Said Paul: "We are troubled on every side, yet not distressed; we are perplexed, but not in despair; Persecuted, but not forsaken; cast down, but not destroyed" (2 Cor. 4:8-9). This is Christian courage. There is no other way to explain it—whether it be in the life of the apostle Paul or in some other brave Christian soldier.

I remember a man of courage who had been in a horrible automobile accident and was first told by his doctors that he would lose the sight of both eyes. Later, they revised the diagnosis and said that while they could save the partial sight of one eye, it would be necessary to remove the other eye and replace it with a glass eye.

As the doctors dropped this heavy missile of bad news upon the patient, they expected to hear weeping, wailing, and the declaration that "life was no longer worth living." Instead, there was a moment of silence and then, with a smile, the injured man said: "Well, doctor, when you take out my eye and replace it with a glass eye, I want you to make certain that the glass eye has a twinkle in it." No one can deny that this kind of invincible attitude is sorely needed in this distressing and discouraging world.

From the famous, bluegrass, horse country of Lexington, Kentucky, there comes an old story of the wealthy race horse owner who bought the "winningest" champion ever to circle a track. Happy to be the proud owner of the very best, he built a new barn and placed this magnificent thoroughbred on display. Over the barn a newly painted sign declared: "THIS IS THE FASTEST HORSE THIS WORLD HAS EVER SEEN."

Tourists drove for miles to get a glimpse of this marvelous animal. One year later the owner entered him again in a race and, much to his chagrin, the horse came in last. Flattened by the disappointment, the owner led him back to the stable and with paintbrush in hand changed the sign to read: "THIS IS THE FAST-EST WORLD THIS HORSE HAS EVER SEEN!"[7]

Some who have not fared too well in the human race can identify with the revision of this sign. Victims of discouragement, they struggle to avoid the pitfalls of bad attitudes.

Why should I even try? can prove to be one of the most fatal questions in the English language. It marks the dividing line between success and failure for countless discouraged human beings. "There's no use in even trying—" is the familiar position of the person who is quick to throw in the towel, almost before the battle begins. It is the sob of the one who wants to avoid work. How much better it would be to use the powerful phrases of courage: You can count on me, and It can be done! These words glow with the light of faith and success.

Gerald Kennedy told of being inspired by a poem entitled "Snow Lilies" which had as its beginning a quotation from a magazine called *Colorado Wild-*

flowers: "The glacier lily or snow lily begins to bloom right at the foot of snowbanks and follows the retreating ice up the mountainside."

This could be applied in terms of that which ought to be the Christian's attitude of courage in what is often a cold, hard world. Strengthened by the warmth of faith, the Christian must keep on growing even in the coldest, hardest circumstances. And this can be done if one remains ever aware of the great resources available to him. We can proclaim with certainty that Jesus Christ can do for us what no one else can. In times of discouragement, we may bemoan our own inadequacy; but at the same time, we must proclaim our Lord's all-sufficiency.

His promise is: Everything that is wrong is going to be made right. Everything that is crooked is going to be made straight. In this truth, we can take courage. When life puts you down, faith in the promises of God can pull you up.

A small girl, who frequently traveled with her parents, was terrified of tunnels. Every time they approached a tunnel, she would close her eyes, press her face against her mother, and refuse to look up until she was assured they had passed through the tunnel and were once again out in the sunshine.

A few years later, to everyone's surprise, her fear had disappeared. Driving along the turnpike, the child was thrilled as they passed through the tunnels. Remembering the child's fear, her mother asked what made the difference. Smiling, the little girl answered, "Mother, I like the tunnels because they have light at both ends."[8]

Discouragement can also have light at both ends: You enter discouragement and exit from discouragement in the light of faith. All the discouragement in the world cannot sink your life if you stay up and remain secure by trusting in the power of Almighty God.

8
But It Hurts!

One who faces life realistically does not seek to hide the grim fact of suffering. It is present wherever there is life.

Many persons know the anguish of daily pain. A young mother of two small children phoned me one afternoon and with halting voice said: "Please . . . pray for me. I have just come from the doctor's office . . . and he could offer no prospect of any lasting relief from my severe back pain."

"I'm sorry to hear that," I said.

"The thing that really gets to me," she continued, "is that I've had surgery and am no better. Apparently there is no real chance of ever getting any better. I feel that I have been sentenced to a life of continuing pain."

When I hung up the phone, I reflected on what she had said: "Sentenced to a life of continuing pain." That is a hard sentence. Still, for a large number of persons, it is one of the realities of life. Poets may write their lines about the joys of eternal youth and the beauty of an unending spring, but you and I know better. *Pain* and *suffering* are the words to authentic sad songs that many are compelled to sing day after day.

Of course, there are some religions that attempt to

deal with pain by denying its existence. But the suffering Christian walks a tightrope, affirming the concern of a loving God while at the same time facing squarely the woeful reality of a pain-wracked body.[1] Even though admitting that the human body is wonderfully made and the nervous system well-engineered, the Christian sufferer may find himself asking the mournful questions: Why must it hurt so much? Is pain a necessary part of life?

Almost as if in answer to the questions, newspapers carried the story of an unusual medical case: an eight-year-old English boy who was always subject to serious injury or death because he could not feel pain. He was a normal boy except that he did not know when he was hurt. For some reason, his nervous system did not signal pain to his brain, and he was required to live in constant peril. Pain does have its place in life. Pain is significant in the total pattern of living.

Dr. Paul Wilson Brand, world-renowned expert on Hansen's disease, says: "Leprosy is called 'the creeping disease' in that people see fingers, toes, hands, and feet slowly vanishing and they are horrified at the patient who pays no attention because he cannot feel the pain."[2]

In his research, the doctor found what he termed "the whole secret of leprosy"—the grotesque deformities are not caused directly by the disease but by the absence of pain. Not feeling pain, a patient puts his hand on a hot stove and it burns away.[3]

The ability to feel pain is a valuable part of life. Pain is essential. Without pain, simple acts like shoveling snow (we could die of unrecognized exhaustion) or taking a bath (we could boil ourselves) would be dangerous. We could destroy ourselves without the built-in protective service provided by the body's warning system.[4]

Pain and suffering also remind us that we need help. When all goes well, man can easily imagine himself as being self-sufficient; but in the trembling throes of suffering, he reaches out in the full realization that God is the necessity for his life.

Like a megaphone, pain gets one's attention. Pain is a leveler of all people. A rock-bottom experience, suffering compels many to consider their lives in the light of eternity and deal with God.

Hence, to recognize pain as a stepping stone and to find the way to bear up under pain that is more than you can bear, we must understand that more important than the fact that people suffer is the manner in which they suffer.

One may break a finger and become bitter and cynical and start clawing at life. In the life of another, there falls pain almost beyond human comprehension in its severity, and yet the recipient of such suffering remains tender, kind, loving, and triumphant. Pain and affliction are bound to color our lives, but we ought to have something to say about the color—whether it shall be a dismal black or a bright and shining gold.

One who colored his suffering in a glowing and victorious manner was described by a minister. He had visited a young man with the dreaded disease of multiple sclerosis. Confined to a specially constructed hospital bed, the young man slowly and painfully spelled

out a message on a set of children's building blocks—
the only means of communication left to him.

For several years he had been fighting a losing battle
with this awful disease which had impaired his vision,
silenced his speech, and partially paralyzed his arms
and legs. For him, his existence was limited to the walls
of his bedroom and regular trips by ambulance to the
hospital.

The visitor at his bedside wondered what word or
words he would spell out as he slowly positioned the
blocks. Was he bitter because of the radical change in
his life? All of his plans, ambitions, and high hopes had
been swept away in a torrent of suffering. The future
had appeared so bright only a few short years before:
He had a lovely home, a wonderful wife, beautiful children, a promising career as a young attorney, and—as
far as he knew then—excellent health.

Now everything was different—well, almost everything. One thing about his life had not changed, his
faith. As the minister watched, the patient's finger
moved from block to block, spelling out two glorious
declarations of faith: "I- A-M- N-O-T- A-F-R-A-I-D. I-
W-O-N-T- G-I-V-E- U-P- T-H-E- F-I-G-H-T!"

For a brief, thoughtful moment, the minister looked
through moist eyes at the heroic message. Although he
had come to minister, he was ministered unto by one
who was meeting the overwhelming odds of illness and
suffering with sweetness of spirit and the steadfastness
of faith. Supported by trusting in God, this young man
continues his courageous fight—bearing up under pain
that is more than he, in his strength alone, could bear.

As the coming of each new day sees his strength wane, so does the ending of each day see his faith enlarged.

The manner in which he suffers is a source of continuing inspiration, as he spelled it out for all of us: Be not afraid. When you face the heavy, ugly, gaping wounds of life, do not fear. Bear up. Dr. Sydnor Stealey, late president of Southeastern Baptist Theological Seminary, put much emphasis on "backbone" when he lectured to young ministers in class at Wake Forest, North Carolina. I can see him now, dark eyes flashing, and voice thundering forth that much-needed word of advice: "Be a man!"

His line of thinking was: Young preacher, if you can't be anything else—if you can't be noted or promoted—recognized or eulogized—you can stand up and be a man! I still feel a tingle and a stiffening of my backbone as I hear those words. This wise old seminary professor was digging down deeply into his own experiences and echoing the words of the apostle Paul: "Watch ye, stand fast in the faith, quit you like men, be strong" (1 Cor. 16:13).

The growing need for obedience to these words is reinforced by the obvious present-day shortage of persons who wear well under the stress, strain, and suffering of life. Someone has asked the question: Where have all of the heroes gone? It is a pertinent question for our day.

The manner in which one faces the trials and trauma of life is of utmost importance. Understand, I am not referring to the tiny pin-pricks of life, but to the real wounds that are deep and purple. Some people stub their toes and make themselves, and everyone around them, miserable. They complain to all who come within earshot. They major on self-pity.

Some persons insist crosses come in all shapes, sizes, and weights, and everyone has his own special cross. If so, it must be readily admitted that the rough, large, heavy crosses are frequently carried more bravely and more gracefully than the smoother, smaller, lighter ones. But enough of this misconception about crosses.

In the Christian sense, if you take up a cross, you take it up willingly as did Jesus our Savior. It is an insult to the sacrificial spirit and attitude of Christ on the Cross for someone with a toothache or a backache to sigh and complain, "Well, I guess it is just my cross to bear!" This cannot be. It is not a "cross" at all, in the truest Christlike sense of the word, unless it is accepted without complaint, declaring in deepest submission, "Not my will, but thine, be done" (Luke 22:42). You remember Jesus said of his life, "No man taketh it from me, but I lay it down of myself" (John 10:18).

Moreover, how foolish it is to compare our sufferings with the excruciating pain endured by our Lord on the Cross for all the sins of mankind. I suspect that we have too often disguised the horrible ugliness of the Cross by allowing it to become a golden trinket at the end of a chain instead of the terrible instrument of execution and death, which it actually was. This much is certain: Knowing in your heart the reality of the suffering of Jesus on the Cross will enable you to face up to pain and endure it with the glad song: "What a friend we have in Jesus,/All our sins and griefs to bear!"

How may we bear up under pain that is more than we can bear? This is the answer: The suffering Christ of the Cross bears all our sin, our pain, and our grief. It was the Christ of the Cross who first showed us the way in his Gethsemane experience as he said what every victorious sufferer must finally come to say: "Nevertheless, not as I will, but God's will be done" (Matt. 26:39, author's translation).

A man related the experience of seeing this degree of submission and surrender take place in the life of a friend. "I saw him die," he said of his friend, "and he was only forty-seven." For seven years the battle for health had raged with the hope that some cure for his disease might be found.

His life had been prolonged with 150 blood transfusions, but this proved to be only a delaying tactic. Death came. All who visited him, even when the pain was at its worst, said he never complained. Following his death his wife, who had stood at his bedside through the trying years, recalled that seven years before when her husband's illness had been diagnosed as Hodgkin's disease, they faced the inevitable.

Doctors at first had given him only six months to live. As life collapsed all about them, they were driven to their knees in fervent prayer and came to the firm resolve to put everything in the hands of God. A short time before his death, his wife asked him: "Darling, in all of this, have you ever felt that God was unjust in permitting you to suffer?"

He thought for only a brief moment before he answered: "If this is the way God wants it, then this is the way I want it."

In a roll call of history's dauntless sufferers, you will discover that this attitude was a source of their inner strength. It was true with the apostle Paul. Beaten and battered by life, in constant danger of assault from his enemies and persecutors, Paul could exclaim: "Most gladly therefore will I rather glory in my infirmities, that the power of Christ may rest upon me" (2 Cor. 12:9).

Paul had learned that God permits suffering to come into the lives of his children not to defeat them but that they might use it to become stronger in the faith. Pain can become a stepping stone to the higher way of complete trust. As Job 23:10 declares: "He knoweth the way that I take: when he hath tried me, I shall come forth as gold."

Hard experiences of life can be refined into gold. A seminary student learned this truth as he struggled through the dark shadows of doubt. His father, serving as pastor of a metropolitan church, was felled by a serious illness which threatened blindness. In his fever-ish delirium, the father said again and again, "Let the precious will of Jesus be done." Even as this was being said, doubt raged in the minister's son who sat at his bedside. How could the loss of an eye, an incapaci-tating illness, and the necessity of a faithful pastor giving up his work, be "the precious will of Jesus"?

Months passed and the scene changed. The father was called as pastor of a rural church and later he was chosen "Rural Pastor of the Year" in his state. All denominations recognized the outstanding job he had done in leading his struggling congregation to innovative avenues of service. Still later, his area of influence was extended through a far-reaching radio ministry. All things had come together in a beautiful pattern of greater achievement for God, and it had all begun with a taxing experience that proved to be a stepping stone to new levels of progress.

As frequently happens, when we are tried, we come forth as gold. Many ministers who have known suffering are quick to agree that they have done their finest preaching after their Gethsemane experiences. It is a law of life. When an irritating grain of sand gets into an oyster, it may make a pearl out of it. Paul did the same with his "thorn in the flesh"—he made a jewel out of it.

Suffering does have its benefits. Pain does have its pluses. If graciously accepted, suffering gives one a clearer sense of values. Under the influence of pain, the things we thought important fade into insignificance, and the things we neglected take on added meaning. Suffering also teaches us the greater value of spiritual values in comparison to things that are merely material. As a stepping stone, the pain that is very hard on our bodies may be very good for our souls. When we are healthy and well and on our feet, we see all around us the glory of the things that shall change and decay. But when we are suffering with the confinement of illness, we find it easier to look up and see the glory of God.

The mother of nine children lay dying. Her devoted husband and children were with her through each day of her terminal illness. The daughter, who was a nurse, gave the necessary injections to alleviate the pain. From a nearby city, the doctor son-in-law came for a visit each week. This close-knit family could only watch the wasted form of this loved one grow weaker, as she drew nearer to the final moment.

One day as their minister was visiting in the home, this dear mother called him to her bedside and said, "Pastor, will you pray with me each day about the matter that is on my heart?"

"Of course," agreed the pastor, thinking that perhaps her prayerful pleas would be for healing or for release from pain.

"Pray, Pastor," she insisted, "pray that my children may never doubt the goodness of God because they see me suffer. Pastor, this I know: God is good."

It was almost as if she were enacting the words of the psalmist: "The Lord is good to all: and his tender mercies are over all his works" (Ps. 145:9). She moved toward the sunset in triumphant faith, as did the mother who, also sensing that her time was short, wrote this inspiring letter to her children:

To my beloved children,

I particularly felt the need and urgency of writing to each one of you and sharing with you some of the deep things on my heart.

First of all, I am asking you to release me entirely to God. I am ready to go and be with Him and how very real and close heaven is to me. For sometimes as I pray, I have to open my eyes to see if Christ is not visibly by my bedside.

Of course, underlying all we say and do, we pray constantly to be in His will and nothing above this. This disease is so devastating that all of us have suffered much during the past two years—mentally, physically, emotionally, and even financially as the prolonged illness takes its terrible toll.

I want you to know that if God does see best to come for me soon, I want you to know that my heavenly Father has allowed me to meet all my goals, and I have had a wonderful time.

> Unbounded love,
> Mother[5]

Bearing up under pain that is more than you can humanly bear is to say once again with Paul: "Most gladly therefore will I rather glory in my infirmities, that the power of Christ may rest upon me" (2 Cor. 12:9). When do you suppose Paul wrote the joyful words, "Rejoice in the Lord alway: and again I say, Rejoice" (Phil. 4:4)? He wrote them when he sat in prison waiting for release or execution. When do you suppose the psalmist wrote, "I will lift up mine eyes unto the hills, from whence cometh my help. My help cometh from the Lord, which made heaven and earth" (Ps. 121:1-2)? I would not be surprised to hear him say in heaven someday that he wrote this passage while he was marching the dark and lonely miles of pain, his face wet with tears, but his heart looking up to God.

Life can be compared to a journey through a dark cavern. Always for those with sturdy faith, there is light up ahead. Walking beside them, holding their hands, is

Jesus the Savior who knows what it is to suffer. Not only did Jesus know the pain of the Cross but also he knew the pain of sorrow as he wept at the grave of Lazarus and cried out in grief over the inhabitants of Jerusalem, who had rejected his salvation. Throughout his earthly ministry, our Lord knew the intense pain of agonizing hours and days. Because of this Jesus can be and is the understanding, sympathizing Savior.

One young woman of devout faith said, "Pastor, my husband and I have decided that we shall not ask the 'why?' until we are ushered into the presence of our Lord, who can give us the answer." These words of absolute trust came from the lips of a wife and mother after she had passed through a great tragedy. Here was faith in the midst of suffering which is the appropriate stance for the child of God. We may not understand why crushing events take place in our lives, but we must continue to entrust the situation to our heavenly Father. He is our Good Shepherd who walks with us through the shadows. And never forget this: It is better to walk in the shadows with him than in the sunshine without him.

A bit of supportive verse in Mary Gardner Brainard's poem "Faith and Sight" says:

> So I go on, not knowing,—I would not, if
> I might—
> I would rather walk in the dark with God
> Than go alone in the light;
> I would rather walk with Him by faith
> Than walk alone by sight.[6]

Make certain as you pass through trial and pain and suffering that you accept the invitation of our Lord: "Come unto me, all ye that labour and are heavy laden, and I will give you rest" (Matt. 11:28).

In sharing a personal experience, Ben C. Fisher, former executive director of the Education Commission of the Southern Baptist Convention, stated, "The power of the gospel is the power to save us from human tragedy." Sometime ago a surgeon sat on the side of Fisher's hospital bed and, in a gentle and considerate manner, told him that he had a deep-seated malignancy. Suspended between shock and disbelief, Fisher struggled to absorb the doctor's words. Cancer is something that happens to someone else, isn't it? Continuing, the surgeon informed him that with further surgery a few more years of life could be possible. But when the doctor left the hospital room and Fisher was alone, with only the audible sound of his own thoughts, he made a wonderful discovery: Whether he had a few months or a few years left, he could live without fear or anxiety.

"In Christ," he said, "I knew that I had the ultimate future and could always abound in hope."

This is God's guarantee, his wonderful warranty in Christ that life need not be a nightmare, that there is never a twilight of the soul, and that no suffering child of God has to wander alone and helpless in the wasteland of pain.

Discharged from the hospital for a time at home, Ben had an opportunity to visit the little mountain cemetery where for more than two hundred years his people have been laid to rest. Walking over to the well-worn tombstone that leaned slightly over the ancient grave site of his great-great-grandfather, he read these words: "These are they that came out of the great tribulation, and are washed in the blood of the Lamb."

Coming down the mountain, Ben reflected on the lives of all the departed saints buried there. He thought of their beliefs, their commitment. They had lived and died in the faith. Near the foot of the mountain, he noticed an inscription which he had never seen before—words which spoke of faith for the future and the presence of hope:

> The Shepherd will come for His sheep,
> And the valley will bloom again.

And so shall it be for all of us, as we, in faith, bear up under pain that is more than we can bear. We, ourselves, are borne in the arms of the Good Shepherd who loves and cares for his sheep.

9
Highjumping the Hurdles

If a sidewalk survey were taken in which all persons who appear to be burdened and bothered were questioned, the interviewer doubtless would hear many moan that, for them, "life was like running an obstacle course." In support of this feeling of futility, Arthur Bloch wrote a book, *Murphy's Law and Other Reasons Things Go Wrong.* Murphy's Law is basic to the old what's-the-use? attitude. It states simply, "If anything can go wrong, it will."

Regrettably, this is the attitude of many who believe that: "Everything put together falls apart sooner or later." They have not yet won their wings of faith which would enable them to leap over the obstacles surrounding them. For example, at a dinner party several persons gathered in a circle and started talking about what they wanted in life. A businessman said: "I just want a business deal to go my way for a change." A father said: "I want our children to do *something right.*" A deeply troubled woman said: "I want to have what it takes to make it in life." Many persons can identify with these desires, and others can look back through the pages of this book and claim a familiarity with all of the obstacles with which we have dealt: trouble, defeat, depression, loneliness, sorrow, impatience, discouragement, and pain.

The question is: Can these obstacles become stepping stones? Well, can they? Obstacles we have, in what seems to be unlimited supply. But what can we do about them? We can start by noting that one of the most important words in the English language is the conjunction *but*. We may have many problems, *but* it is good to be alive and attempting to solve them. We may have more than our share of trials, adversities, and obstacles, *but* we have many blessings for which to be grateful.

A newspaper filler declared: An ostrich is unable to fly, *but* can outrun most birds in flight. And a bee can never be an eagle, *but* it can make honey. The conjunctions of life remind us that nature has a way of compensating for some weaknesses. In fact, I heard of one positive thinker who believed that nature compensated for certain flaws: "The blind may have a sharper sense of hearing, the deaf a keener sense of smell." And furthermore, he said he had always noticed that "someone with a shorter leg had a longer one to make up for it."

To overcome obstacles, we need this kind of good humor. I also like the incident concerning the little old lady who, though not blessed with this world's goods and confined for most of her years as an invalid in a wheelchair, possessed a marvelous sense of humor. Her faith was strong, but her health had been so wretched all of her life that she had been unable to attend church often enough to establish her membership. Now she was very old and, having long since professed her Christian faith, she wished to join the local church. Her one good leg had been amputated at the hip and she could not move without her wheelchair. But what a spirit she had! On that day when she was rolled down the aisle and received for church membership, she leaned over to the pastor and with a twinkle in her eye asked: "Does this mean that I will have to give up dancing?"

How very important it is to be able to look up and laugh. Good, honest laughter is essential to the full, contented life. Laughter and joy are integral parts of a healthy personality.

In one of his sermons, Peter Marshall said: "God is a God of laughter as well as of prayer—a God of singing as well as of tears. God loves to hear us laugh. We do not honor God by our austerity. If God, for you, does not smile, there is something wrong with your idea of God."[1]

And how God must smile at his children who press on in dedicated service despite what some would consider insurmountable obstacles. An example of such dedication takes place every Sunday morning at Emmanuel Baptist Church, Tucson, Arizona, as an ambulance pulls up to the side door, and two attendants unload Al Maynard on a small portable bed. He is then transferred to a two-wheeled pushcart and rolled in to teach his boys' Sunday School class.[2]

Called "a witness on crutches," this middle-aged man is then carted to the main auditorium where he stands on crutches. His prayer inspires the congregation as he prays, "Oh, Lord, give us the strength to do your will." For the past ten years, 95 percent of this man's body has been "frozen" as a result of the ravages of spondylitic arthritis which left his spine in a permanently fixed position. Realizing that this stiffening, freezing process was taking place in his body, Al decided to place boards in his bed so that his spine would be locked in the lying-standing position. Asked why he did not choose the sitting position, he replied with a smile: "So that I can stand for my Lord."[3]

Determination, supported by faith, can overcome obstacles. I saw evidence of this when I was a teenager and joined several friends one summer night to visit with a black congregation in a South Carolina city. Revival services were in progress, and we went to hear the preacher who enjoyed quite a reputation as a great pulpiteer.

The service was lively from music to message, but the high point of the evening came at testimony time. An elderly black woman, well into her eighties, stood and told all who packed the auditorium what faith in God had done for her. Dressed in white, with a crown of silver hair encircling her head, she related her personal experience with the Lord. A dramatic quietness filled the room as her voice reached out to grab the attention of her hearers. Twenty years before she had been crippled with rheumatism, she declared, and was compelled to hobble around on a walking cane to give added support to her weakened legs.

Then something glorious had happened to her. Easing down one day on her aching knees for a talk with God, she cried: "Lord, if it be your sweet will, let power be restored once more to my feeble limbs!" She then got to her feet, saw her walking cane in the corner, pointed her finger and shouted: "Old cane, I'm leaving you!" And, she said, she did just that. She walked away from her cane and never picked it up again. In her faith, she had found a stronger source of support.

From earliest times, people of this world have had obstacles to overcome and with God's assistance they have used barriers as stepping stones. Moses is often spoken of as a shy man, seeking to withdraw from responsibility. But actually this great man of God was reluctant to attempt to lead the children of Israel because he was slow of speech—he stammered.

"Please Lord," he insisted, "I have never been eloquent, neither recently nor in time past, nor since Thou has spoken to Thy servant; for I am slow of speech and slow of tongue" (Ex. 4:10, NASB). Some would have described Moses as "afflicted." But the Lord called him and said: "I made that mouth, and I made all other mouths, and now I will give you a mouth that will speak for you—a mouth that can communicate—the youth of your own brother, Aaron" (Ex. 4:11-15, author's translation). And Moses, clearing this hurdle, went on to lead the children of Israel out of the wilderness.

In recalling heroes of World War II, one dare not exclude Winston Churchill. When Great Britain was almost down for the count and Hitler's arm was poised, ready to be lifted as victor, the stirring voice of Churchill—a speaker who literally changed the course of human history—rallied his people and sent them back to the battle. Few realized that his unusual speaking ability was not a style but an affliction. Churchill stammered throughout his life, making him sound the way he did. Subsequent events proved that the affliction he never completely corrected became a stepping stone to greatness.

Who has not known people who have grown larger in usefulness as a result of their difficulties? We may learn something from the mountain brook which takes the stones in its path as the instruments which enable it to sing. The obstacles make the songs. Songs are oftentimes born of hardship. The echoing music of the world is but the cumulative testimony of men and women who, with divine help, have run through and leaped over their obstacles.

In any enumeration of handicaps and obstacles, we would do well to remember that both British Admiral Nelson and French emperor Napoleon were relatively small men. Alexander the Great, despite his high-sounding name, was a hunchback. Aesop, brilliant writer of fables, was deformed. Milton was blind. Composer Beethoven and inventor Thomas Edison were deaf, and Helen Keller was deaf, mute, and blind. Author Robert Louis Stevenson, who thrilled the world with the classics that flowed from his pen, said before his death in 1894 that he had never known a day of good health.

Call the roll of all these who achieved greatness and they would report that they looked beyond their obstacles and stepped over them. And all such conquerors of handicaps are not in the past. Wayne Dehoney tells of a conversation he had with Mrs. Marse

Grant, wife of the editor of the North Carolina Baptist paper. Mrs. Grant, happily anticipating having all of her children home for Thanksgiving, said: "We have three daughters. Two are married. And then, there is the youngest daughter—let me tell you about our youngest daughter. She works for the state with the physically handicapped. She is just the joy of our life—one of those bubbling, happy persons for whom every day is filled with happiness."

"That's wonderful," Dehoney said, "I'm sure she enjoys her work."

"Yes," said Mrs. Grant, "here—I have a picture of her."

Dehoney took the picture and was surprised by what he saw: She had been a thalidomide baby and the deformities were obvious: She stood about four feet tall, with only hands extended from her shoulders, body supported by a brace, and twisted legs steadied by braces to enable her to walk.

"How does she manage?" he asked.

"Oh," said the proud mother, "she just does wonderfully. She has her own house and washes dishes with her feet because her arms cannot reach around and make contact. She drives her own specially built automobile—she is the most independent person and the happiest child we have.[4]

This young woman has leaped over her obstacles. She is happy, appreciates life, and is thankful to God for every day she lives. Through grateful eyes, she sees blessings in the midst of difficulties. With many, the reverse is true: they do not see the blessings because their eyes are focused on the problems.

It was so with Elisha's servant in the Old Testament episode when the Syrian king attempted to capture the prophet at Dothan, north of Samaria (2 Kings 6:8-19). With chariots and an army, the Syrians surrounded the city at night. In the early morning fog, Elisha's servant heard the fearsome sound of rumbling chariots, the neighing of war horses, the clatter of armor, and shouted military orders. The whole scene was frightening, and he ran as fast as he could to get the old prophet. "Oh, Master," he cried in alarm, "what shall we do?" Elisha pondered the situation for a moment and then reassured his servant with the words: "They that be with us are more than they that be with them" (v. 16).

Surely, thought the servant, the old man must be mad. Then Elisha prayed, "Lord, open his eyes that he may see." The fog on the Samaritan hills lifted and the mountains behind Dothan were covered with fiery chariots and horses—God's army! What appeared at first to be an unconquerable obstacle turned out on closer look to be the revealed blessings and strength of God. If we are to move along the precarious roads of life, we must not be blind to that power which equips us to overcome our hardships.

J. Harold Smith says: "Obstacles are those frightful things you see when you take your eyes off the goal."[5] Studies of the history and development of successful men disclose that those at the top had a constant struggle to get there. There was no magic formula or easy road to success. The journey was one detour after another and all uphill.

Some students of personal achievement maintain that if you single out one trait which separates men at the top from those milling around the bottom, it would be this: The real achievers in life are success-oriented and have an instinct which allows them to regard all obstacles as simply a normal part of their travel. They are never distracted or turned back by adversity. Instead they double their efforts when faced with large problems and invariably keep their eyes on their goals and objectives. Tenaciously, they keep on, not willing to give up the struggle.

The following words by an unknown author are the battle cry of all dedicated individuals who leap over their obstacles:

> I won't let go!
> I want to let go, but I won't let go.
> There are battles to fight,
> By day and by night,
> For God and the right—
> And I'll never let go.
>
> I want to let go, but I won't let go.
> I'm sick, 'tis true,
> Worried and blue,
> And worn through and through,
> But I won't let go.
>
> I want to let go, but I won't let go.
> I will never yield!

What? Lie down on the field
And surrender my shield?
No, I'll never let go!

I want to let go, but I won't let go.
May this be my song
"Mid legions of wrong—
Oh, God, keep me strong
That I may never let go!"

Perseverance is one of the crowning virtues of sturdy saints, along with the ability to make the best of the worst. In other words, make the most of your blessings, your assets, and your joyful moments; make the least of your handicaps, your liabilities, and your obstacles. Make the most of your opportunities, your talents, and your successes; make the least of your difficulties, your limitations, and your failures. Make the most of your achievement; make the least of your adversity.

Your view of life is one of the utmost importance. It spells the difference between being crushed by obstacles or leaping over them. And the truth is, in most instances, we see what we want to see. A vulture soaring in the air is unmindful of the beauty of flowers, grass, and trees. He sees only a dead rabbit under a bush because it is that for which he is looking. One man looks at a glass of water, and says it is half-empty. Another, seeing the same glass, says it is half-full. Both the beautiful and the sordid are in the eyes of the beholder. One sees what he is seeking. If you look above your obstacles and view the passing scene positively, you will see that life can be beautiful.

In Ezekiel 40:16, we find the picturesque phrase: "And there were narrow windows" which summarizes a condition of contemporary life. Many people make the mistake of looking out on life through narrow windows. They feel the restriction of their circumstances, the oppression of their handicaps and difficulties. Assuming that the great tide of life has come in, gone out again, and left them stranded, they peer through narrow windows, waiting to pick a quarrel with life. So much depends upon our point of view. One person looks out of the window and sees a beautiful green meadow. Another looks and sees only the dirt on the window.

With gratitude we can say that some of the grandest work being done for God is carried on by men and women who are forced to look at life through the narrow windows of restricted circumstances. Because they are people of vision and faith, they see beyond the circumstances to the joy on the other side of the hill.

In an interview with *Christianity Today,* Madeleine L'Engle, writer of children's books, said: "Perhaps the reason I always had a deep sense of the nearness of a personal God was the influence of a marvelous old English woman who took care of me. She was a true Christian saint. Wherever she was, there was laughter and joy. Yet, she had a terrible life. Her husband was a total alcoholic. She had to take her children's Sunday coats with her to work; otherwise, her husband hocked them for booze. She quite often didn't know where the money would be for the rent. In later years she suffered with painful arthritis. But she always brought laughter with her."[6] Confronted by obstacles, some despair—others have joy in spite of all the bad scenes that life brings forth. For happiness usually depends on what we see when we look out of our narrow windows. And what we see largely depends upon our faith in God.

It is indicative of our times to say that although many of the new homes constructed in recent years have large picture windows, the views of some of the occupants of those houses are becoming smaller. Reflect on it: Windows are getting larger, but views are becoming smaller. We are looking more and seeing less. And the truth is, we cannot have the larger view of life unless we see all things in the perspective of a personal faith in God.

The secret of overcoming obstacles and enjoying personal assurance is to believe in God—not as a distant ruler of the universe—but as a father, a father who loves us and cares for us as only our heavenly Father can. This permits us to step over our obstacles and gratefully live each day. Wisdom for day-to-day living is reflected in the old sampler on the wall of a colonial farmhouse: "Yesterday is dead; leave it. Tomorrow may never come; don't worry. Today is here; live it!" Taking each day as it comes should be classified under the heading of "good common sense." As disturbing as the past was, and as hectic as the future may be, it must be said that "he who keeps one eye on the past and one eye on the future will be cockeyed in the present." In spite of obstacles that crowd our path, living one day at a time in the strength of God makes every day worth living.

A man on a hiking trip through the Blue Ridge Mountains came to the top of a hill and saw, just below the crest, a small log cabin. The aged owner of the rustic structure was sitting in front of the door, puffing on a corncob pipe. When the traveler drew close enough, he asked the old man patronizingly: "Lived here all of your life?"

"Nope," the old mountaineer replied patiently. "Not yet."

However long or short life may be, there is time for us to live our days in the strength and purpose of God.

Professor Alfred N. Whitehead of Harvard was widely recognized as a deep thinker. Asked the essence of his own complicated thought on faith, the noted scholar said: "Abide with me: fast falls the eventide; the darkness deepens; Lord, with me abide!" In all things, the abiding presence of our Lord makes the difference. Missionary David Livingstone, on furlough from his mission station in Africa and speaking on a university campus said: "Would you have me tell you why I went to Africa and have labored there among the earth's savages, amidst the perils of wilderness?

"It was simply this: the Lord's unfailing promise, ' . . . and, lo, I am with you alway, even unto the end of the world' " (Matt. 28:20). This is the reality of the sustaining power of our Lord, enabling one to rise above hardships by the grace of a loving Lord. Here is that eternal truth expressed by Annie Johnson Flint:

> God hath not promised
> Skies always blue,

Flower-strewn pathways
All our life through;
God hath not promised
Sun without rain,
Joy without sorrow,
Peace without pain.

But God hath promised
Strength for the day,
Rest for the labor,
Light for the way,
Grace for the trials,
Help from above,
Unfailing sympathy,
Undying love.[7]

Through the ages, man in his experiences has verified the reliability of God's promises.

Shortly before his death, Bishop Arthur J. Moore summarized the victorious life of faith in these beautiful words: "We march, not toward the setting sun, but toward the light of morning; the light that shineth more and more unto the perfect day." With that kind of attitude, we can look even at tragedy through the eyes of faith. We can face the worst because we believe the best. Obstacles then become opportunities; millstones become milestones; troubles are something to grow on, and problems are seen not as stumbling blocks but stepping stones.

"And he spake unto the children of Israel, saying, When your children shall ask their fathers in time to come, saying, What mean these stones? Then ye shall let your children know, saying, Israel came over this Jordan on dry land" (Josh. 4:21-22). Obviously, in light of the theme on which I have written, I have referred to stones which speak as loudly of faith as the stones that commemorated the safe passage of the Israelites across the Jordan River.

What mean the stones of defeat, depression, sorrow, pain, and discouragement? With triumphant faith in God, they can mean stepping stones. The same loving God, who dried up the swollen Jordan for the crossing of the children of Israel, is able to bring us through the river of our difficulties—allowing us to enter the Promised Land on stepping stones that lead to the ever brighter day.

NOTES

Chapter 1

1. *Time Magazine,* September 4, 1978, p. 67.

2. *Quote,* August 6, 1978, p. 122.

3. Richard Armour, *Quote,* September 3, 1978, p. 219.

4. Donald K. Paulson, *The Messenger,* First Baptist Church, Roanoke, Ala., May 7, 1978.

5. Ibid.

6. Kennedy, Gerald, *A Reader's Notebook* (New York: Harper & Brothers, 1953), p. 307.

7. W. Clyde Tilley, *Open Windows* (Nashville: Sunday School Board, October, 1978).

Chapter 2

1. *Quote Magazine* (Anderson, S.C., July 2, 1978), p. 3.

2. *Quarterly Review,* October, 1973, p. 21.

3. Ibid.

4. Ibid.

5. The Rev. Melvin D. McIntosh, *Minister's Forum,* The News-Herald, Morganton, North Carolina, March 31, 1978.

6. Ibid.

7. *Pulpit Helps,* Chattanooga, Tennessee, AMG International, November, 1978.

Chapter 3

1. Dr. J. Harold Smith, *Quote,* November 12, 1978.

2. Worrell, George E., *Resources for Renewal* (Nashville: Broadman Press), 1975, p. 138.

3. *Quote* (Sunshine Magazine), July 10, 1978, p. 10.

4. *The Christian Index,* sermon by R. J. Robinson, June 13, 1974, p. 4.

Chapter 4

1. Charles L. Allen, *In Quest of God's Power* (Fleming H. Revell Company), *Quote,* February 20, 1966, Volume 51, Number 8, p. 8.

2. John Claypool, "Owning Our Needs," *The Quarterly Review* (Nashville: The Baptist Sunday School Board, October, November, December, 1978), p. 14.

3. Ibid.

4. *Baptist and Reflector* (Tennessee Baptist Convention, March 6, 1975), p. 2.

5. *Pulpit Digest,* September, 1967, pp. 25, 26.

6. Ibid.

7. *The Baptist Program,* March, 1978, p. 5.

8. *Christianity Today,* "Eutychus VIII," April 7, 1978, p. 8.

Chapter 5

1. Norman Vincent Peale, *Quote Magazine* (Anderson, S.C., June 27, 1965), p. 6.

2. Wayne Dehoney, *The Pulpit of Walnut Street Baptist,* February 19, 1978.

3. Ibid.

4. *Interpreter's Bible* (Nashville: Abingdon Press), Volume IV, p. 210.

5. *Banner-Herald, The Daily News* (Athens, Ga., November 5, 1978), p. 13.

6. *Christianity Today* (Carol Stream, Ill., March 24, 1978), p. 8.

Chapter 7

1. Ben Haden, *Changed Lives,* Chattanooga, Tennessee, C. 1976, p. 5.

2. Lowell, M. Atkinson, *Pulpit Digest,* September-October, 1975, Manhasset, New York, p. 45.

3. Charles H. Mayo, *Quote Magazine* (Anderson, S.C., June 13, 1965), Volume 49, Number 24, p. 13.

4. *The Pulpit,* Walnut Street Baptist Church, Louisville, Kentucky, October 22, 1978.

5. Sam Ervin, *Quote* (Anderson, S.C., February 9, 1975), p. 129.

6. Ibid.

7. *Proclaim* (Nashville: Sunday School Board, January, 1979), p. 30.

8. Ed Young, *Pulpit Helps,* reprinted from *Minister's Manual* (New York: Harper & Row, 1978).

Chapter 8

1. Philip Yancey, "Pain: The Tool of the Wounded Surgeon," *Christianity Today* (Washington, D. C., March 24, 1978), p. 12.

2. *People Weekly* (Chicago, Ill., February 13, 1978), Volume 9, Number 6, p. 69.

3. Ibid.

4. Yancey.

5. B. David Edens, "Family Living," *Baptist and Reflector,* Nashville, Tennessee, April 18, 1979.

6. Mary Gardner Brainard, *Masterpieces of Religious Verse* (Nashville: Broadman Press, 1977), p. 384.

Chapter 9

1. Catherine Marshall, *A Man Called Peter* (New York: McGraw-Hill Book Company, Inc., 1951), p. 138.

2. Jack Gulledge, "A Witness on Crutches," *The Sunday School Builder* (Nashville: Sunday School Board, May, 1964), p. 12.

3. Ibid.

4. Wayne Dehoney, *The Pulpit,* Walnut Street Baptist Church, Louisville, Kentucky, November 20, 1977.

5. *Quote* (Anderson: Droke Publishing House, October 22, 1978), p. 385.

6. Philip Yancey, *Christianity Today* (Washington, D.C., June 8, 1979), p. 15.

7. *Proclaim* (Nashville: Sunday School Board, July, 1978), Volume 8, Number 4, p. 10.